"Crony capitalism has been the
From the destructive mercantile
boondoogles of the 19th century to wasteful infrastructure projects of the
20th century, to the inefficient green industries of today, government-
business partnerships have been supplanting the vibrant spirit of
entrepreneurial enterprise with the dead hand of government bureaucracy.
We've reached the stage in which the wealth-producing economy has been
hollowed out, the legal foundations of society have been perverted, and the
social fabric of our communities have been rend asunder.

Gregg and Jamin Hübner have done a remarkable service in chronicling
the devastation wrought by wind farms, or as they aptly call them wind
industrial parks, to their beloved South Dakota. For those of us who share
their love of the Great Plains, let us hope that their struggle has attained more
than a stay of execution."

_—JEFFREY HERBENER, Ph.D_
_Economics Department Chair, Grove City College_

"This is an extremely informative book and likely to become a must-read for
anyone that lives around or is considering allowing a wind farm on their
property. As a physician, a person intensely interested in the environment,
and a person with an undergraduate degree in wildlife biology, I found this
book very helpful."

_—THOMAS RIES, M.D._

"At present, wind energy is a losing proposition for all but those developers
that benefit from government subsidization of their industry. Hubner gives
an accessible overview of how and why this is truly the case."

_—NORMAN HORN, Ph.D_
_Engineering Post-Doc, MIT_

# PARADISE DESTROYED

## THE DESTRUCTION OF RURAL LIVING
## BY THE WIND ENERGY SCAM

GREGG HUBNER

*Assisted by*

JAMIN HÜBNER

Printed in the United States of America

Cover photo by Jamin Hübner, taken in southwestern Minnesota near Sioux Falls, South Dakota

ISBN-13: 978-0-9905943-3-8
ISBN-10: 0990594335

BISAC Subject Headings:
      BUS099000 BUSINESS & ECONOMICS / Environmental Economics
      BUS094000 BUSINESS & ECONOMICS / Green Business
      BUS070040 BUSINESS & ECONOMICS / Industries / Energy
      BUS036050 BUSINESS & ECONOMICS / Investments & Securities / Real Estate

# About the Author

**Gregg C. Hubner** grew up on a farm north of Avon, South Dakota and presently lives a mile south of there with his wife of forty-two years, Marsha (Littau) Hubner. He went to country school through the eighth grade and graduated from Avon High School in 1969. He attended the National College of Business and South Dakota State University. For the first sixteen years of their marriage they ran a farm and ranch supply store. They also built a convenience store and ran it for two years. He has been an auctioneer since 1970, a Real Estate Broker in South Dakota since 1983, and a Certified General Appraiser since 1992.

Gregg and Marsha have four children and seven grandchildren. For the last thirty-four years, they have been in the real estate business, including brokerage, auctions and appraisals, along with farming their own land. In 2012, they built a new "retirement" home that is now jeopardized by the wind farm scam.

# About the Assistant Author

**Dr. Jamin Hübner** is the youngest of Gregg and Marsha's four children. He is a graduate of Dordt College (BA), Reformed Theological Seminary (MA), the University of South Africa (ThD), and is currently a graduate student for Southern New Hampshire University (MS). In addition to running several small businesses with his wife Jessica, he serves as the General Editor of the *Christian Libertarian Review*, and the Director of Institutional Effectiveness and part-time professor of economics at John Witherspoon College in the Black Hills.

# TABLE OF CONTENTS

305 ft

550 ft

# ACKNOWLEDGEMENTS

This book is the result of nearly three years of trying to educate people about wind energy and the scam that it is. It is the culmination of meetings, letters to the editor, news articles, conversations and, unfortunately at times, heated confrontations that I have experienced over that time.

This project would not have come to completion without the essential help of others. I want to first thank my wife, Marsha, who has been by my side through this battle and many more. She has been supportive and at times critical, but never once has wavered.

I also need to thank Winnie Peterson from Lincoln County, SD. Winnie is the chairperson for WE-CARE South Dakota and has had the insight to build a large, local non-profit organization in Lincoln County to educate the public and save her community, which have been my goals as well. She presented the first meeting in my home and brought a car load of people to testify at the PUC meeting in Avon.

I also thank Ed Van Gerpen, a former state legislator who has made countless trips to Pierre and made presentations to the county officials. Ed is very community minded and wants to save our great place to live.

I thank Jamin, my son, for helping write, revise, and publish this book—especially for writing most of chapters three and nine.

And thanks to all of the people that have supported us with letters to the editor, emails, and those that testified at the PUC meeting in Avon. Again, thank you.

The most rewarding thing in all of this is when an elderly, former neighbor said to me, "Gregg, I completely changed my mind on wind energy after what I have learned from you."

Gregg Hubner
Avon, South Dakota
June, 2017

# — Introduction —

Growing up in South Dakota, I have always had a love for the land—rural living in particular.

One of my fondest memories in those earlier years was when Mom would bring lunch to the field. We would shut down the tractors, sit on the bare ground and have a picnic of that great home cooked food, or sometimes a summer sausage sandwich, some cake and coffee. It was quiet. The air was fresh. Everything was peaceful.

Today, the younger generation usually ends up in the city, but there is a growing number of young families that want to live in the country or a small town. Because of travels in my business, I have been blessed over the years to see a lot of country. South Dakota is a beautiful state. For us that live in the country, we have access all day long to God's wonderful creation. We can see the sunrise and the sunset. We can wake up to the sights and sounds of pheasants, deer, turkeys, cattle and especially the song birds. The people in the rural areas of our country live in a "Paradise." Our state government tries to entice young people to stay in the state by trying to provide jobs and amenities in the smaller communities, but at the same time, I see the rural areas being destroyed by a taxpayer scam called "Wind Energy."

My grandfather lost the family farm in the Great Depression. My dad has told the story to me growing up how Grandpa cried like a baby when he was able to buy it back from the insurance company he lost it to. Since then, the land became even more precious, and the utmost in stewardship was expected from each generation going forward.

### The Truth About Wind Energy

What you will learn in the following pages is that common perceptions of wind energy are profoundly mistaken.

Despite the name, "wind farms" are not farms. They are industrial electricity-generating factories. They do not store anything—whether wind or electricity. The wind turbines are also not "windmills." At an incredible 400 to 550 feet tall, they are more like rotating skyscrapers. The wind developers are not as they claim, "your friends and neighbors." They are mostly out-of-state developers that will never live near a wind turbine or on a "wind farm" themselves. The actual owners will never live near a wind turbine, either.

Nearly all of the investors will never live near a wind turbine. Why not? For the simple fact that no one in their right mind would build a new home anywhere close to a 500 foot-tall wind turbine—nearly 80% taller than the Statue of Liberty. However, in a sick twist of property rights, developers *can* legally build a 550 ft. wind turbine 1000 ft. from *your* home.

Another myth is that wind projects are built with integrity, honesty, and public transparency. In reality, wind energy is a case of crony-capitalism—where capitalists collude with the government to give themselves and their projects an unfair advantage. When a wind project is unveiled in an area, by the time the local people get educated on what is really happening, the county officials have done everything in their power to help the developer. Furthermore, the county is promised money. The school is promised money. The unsuspecting landowner is promised money. Developers project all of this money by projecting calculations that look 25 to 50 years into the future. And with numbers so big, how could anyone turn it down?

Once this monetary bait is dropped, developers pressure landowners to sign a lease with a confidentiality clause so that once it's signed, they'd better not complain. They also better not tell their neighbor how much they're getting paid. Ultimately, the privacy and peace of landowners was just sold to someone they don't even know.

The developers, in turn, can transfer the rights to *whomever* they want and *as many times* as they want. In fact, the lease will probably outlast its own signer. The wind towers will almost certainly be there longer than you or I—turning or not turning. At the very least, signers of such agreements can expect to see total strangers cross their land for the next thirty years.

The whole topic concerns a variety of different areas, including property rights. But, many readers may be thinking: "if the turbines aren't on your land, what right do you have for objecting to it?" This is a good question. We need to be reminded about how property rights work. Judge Andrew Napolitano illustrates the issue:

> If you lived in a very crowded area, would the government be justified in preventing you from blaring extraordinarily loud music at midnight, or at least requiring you to pay 'damages' to your neighbors for doing so? Certainly, by playing obnoxious music, you are diminishing your neighbors' natural right to the use and enjoyment of their property. And over time, if you were habitually noisy, then it most likely would decrease the market value of their property. Thus, although the government could not criminalize this kind of expression, it would be more than justified in making it actionable, or in other words, the basis for lawsuit.[1]

People can do whatever they want with their property—*so long as it doesn't infringe on the person or properties of others.* The rights of property owners are only violated if someone has substantially infringed on their right to enjoy their property.[2] It is not enough to simply say "not in my backyard" ("NIMBY"), unless there really is some infringement.

So the question is, do wind farms substantially and negatively affect people's enjoyment of their property? Does it decrease the value of their property because wind turbines are built near or on their property? This book will answer with a resounding *"yes."* The local complaints about wind energy *are* justified.

Before going any further, I should also say that I am not against renewable energy. I am *for* renewable energy—but renewable energy that stands on its own feet. This immediately rules out contemporary wind energy because of its utter dependence on government subsidies and tax

---

[1] Andrew Napolitano, *It's Dangerous to be Right When the Government is Wrong* (Nashville: Thomas Nelson, 2011), 48.
[2] For a history of this common law of "private nuisance," and how it became compromised by concern for "public interest," see Sean Coyle and Karen Morrow, *The Philosophical Foundations of Environmental Law: Property, Rights, and Nature* (Portland: Hart Publishing, 2004).

credits. Wind energy also cannot compete with other energy forms because *the wind doesn't blow all the time.*

This a very simple concept, but it is a notorious logistical problem that has plagued the wind industry from the very beginning. Large amounts of electricity cannot be stored. Any interruption in the supply of wind is an interruption in the supply of electricity. This is why the wind turbines are usually only 30% to 40% efficient. (It would be like a farmer buying two or three combines, but only one does the work while the rest just sit there!) Wind turbines simply cannot compete with any coal or natural gas generating plants because as soon as the wind calms down, the other resources have to be there to pick up the slack.

What does this mean? It means that wind is not an "alternative" source of energy; *it is an intermittent supplemental energy.* That's a big difference, and it means that the rhetoric of the whole topic is misleading from the start.

### Wind Energy in South Dakota—and Beyond

Finding sound, clean sources of energy is important for any society.

But what is even more important is the immediate protection of residents and this priceless place we have called the rural Midwest. This is the job of the county zoning board and the county commissioners. Their job, we should be reminded, is to *protect their residents and ensure their property rights are being respected.* This should be far more important than making money for wind energy developers and investors—whether the projects are public or private. But, as we'll learn, this usually isn't the case.

According to the South Dakota Public Utilities Commission website, our state has thirteen wind projects in production along with a few smaller units to total 884 Megawatts (MW). Also on their site are thirty-five proposed wind projects for our state (see the map below).[3]

But we should be reminded that South Dakota is not the only state

---

[3] South Dakota Public Utilities Commission. "South Dakota Wind Energy Development." (August, 2016).
https://puc.sd.gov/commission/Energy/Wind/winddevelopment%20map.pdf
(accessed April, 2017). The second image of Oklahoma comes from thewindfallcoalition.com, and third from the US Department of Energy. energy.gov/maps/map-projected-growth-wind-industry-now-until-2030

being colonized by Big Wind. States like Minnesota have been fighting the movement for over a decade. Now, in 2017, over a dozen states have recently become aware of these developments—and countless residents are fighting tooth and nail against them.

In the pages below, I've included a map of not only South Dakota, but Oklahoma and its projected wind farms. Then, there is a map from the federal energy website of projected wind energy for the whole U.S. by 2030. All of this shows the larger scope of the industry.

As mentioned earlier, we live in an era of "crony capitalism." Powerful corporations and politicians have legislated their way to wealth by passing laws for their own financial benefit. Wind energy is a prime example. Instead of capitalism and a true "free market" where the state simply acts as a referee to establish a level playing field, the government is hi-jacked through politics to hinder competitors and give select businesses an unfair advantage.

If this craze doesn't stop, South Dakota, Oklahoma, Nebraska, Minnesota, Iowa and many other rural states will have eliminated the quality of life for tens of thousands of residents that live in rural areas. This will hurt the states as a whole. People will not move into these areas; they will move *out*. New home construction will plummet. Smaller communities will lose their schools because of declining enrollment. And most obvious, the skyline will be full of wind turbines just like in Spain and Germany. In a word, our beautiful state will be gone.

This book will try to explain why this is happening. Wind energy projects are not like a new car that you buy, don't like, and then trade in for something else. It's not even like marrying the wrong person and settling for a divorce. Once these gigantic concrete and steel structures are built, they are here for generations and generations. For how long, no one actually knows, because we're wading into uncharted territory. I wish our political leaders would understand that, because there is no recourse.

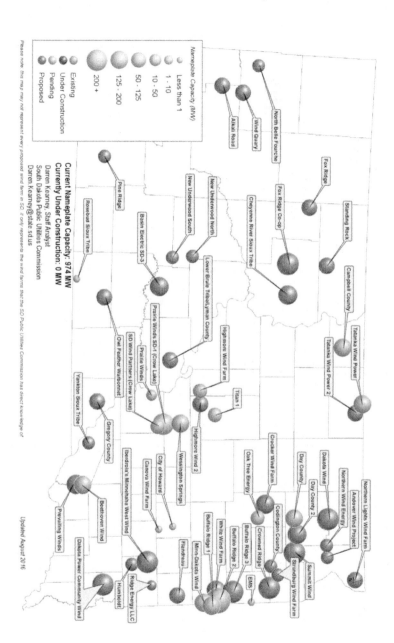

# South Dakota Wind Energy Development

## by Capacity and Status

**Nameplate Capacity (MW)**
- Less than 1
- 1 - 10
- 10 - 50
- 50 - 125
- 125 - 200
- 200 +

Existing
Under Construction
Pending
Proposed

Current Nameplate Capacity: 974 MW
Currently Under Construction: 0 MW
Darren Kearney, Staff Analyst
South Dakota Public Utilities Commission
Darren.Kearney@state.sd.us

Please note this map may not represent every proposed wind farm in SD. If only represents the wind farms that the SD Public Utilities Commission has direct knowledge of

Updated August 2016

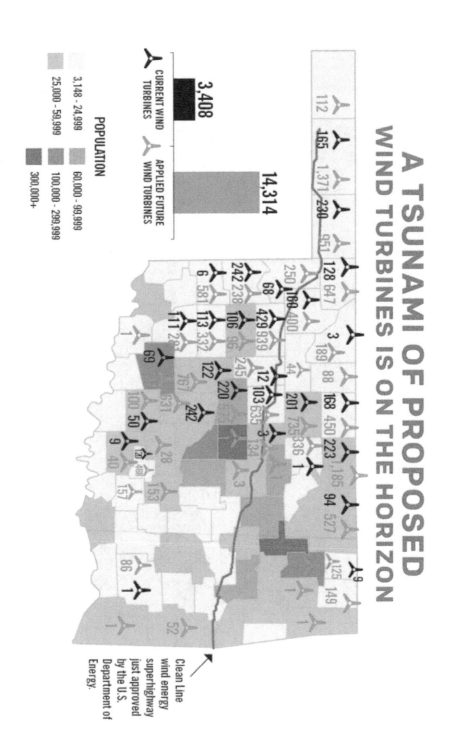

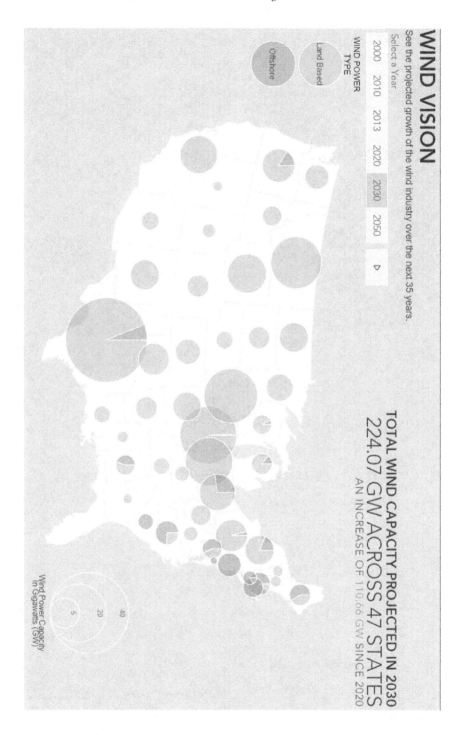

# — 1 —

# MY FIRST LESSON ON WIND ENERGY

Up until February of 2010, all I knew about wind farms is what I saw when driving to Minneapolis every couple years or so. Driving on I-90 going east, I would see clusters of turbines to the north. And a few times when driving north through more turbines and getting as close as maybe a quarter mile, I would sigh and say to myself, "Boy, I'm glad I don't have to live here."

Then, in early 2010, I had the fortunate opportunity to attend a school sponsored by the American Society of Farm Managers and Rural Appraisers as a continuing education class for my real estate broker's and appraiser's licenses. It was presented by Terry A. Argotsinger (AFM, ARA) from Storm Lake, Iowa. This one-day seminar opened up my eyes to the real size, scope and cost of industrial wind farms (although, again, the word "farm" is a bit of misnomer).

### Insights from the Seminar

After a wind project is built, it effectively turns agricultural (and sometimes recreational) land into an industrial park. The whole series of turbines (towers) working together resemble a giant amusement park with flashing red lights at night. The towers are anywhere from 300-550 ft. tall, and the blades have a diameter of 300 to 400 ft., which travel up to 190 mph at the tip of the blades. Developers build these projects anywhere from a handful of turbines to several hundred in a cluster.

The turbines are also noisy—and in more ways than one. There is the obvious *whoosh whoosh whoosh*. But as the wind picks up, the generators at the top of the tower create a "whine" noise. This is a mechanical noise from the generator. Depending how close you are and how many turbines there are, it can be more than just an annoyance. Turbines also produce "infrasound," a low frequency vibration that the body can feel and the brain can detect, but the ears cannot. The effects of this infrasound on the human body is something not yet entirely understood. But there is good reason to believe it isn't positive (more on this later). The effect of this sound on nearby plants and animals is also unverified.

Furthermore, each tower also produces strong seismic vibrations that can travel *miles* through the ground.[4] The steel structure of the tower and the massive 20-35 ft deep concrete foundation are particularly good at conducting noise. Again, the short and long-term effects of this seismic activity on plant growth, wildlife, earthworms, insects, and other life is largely a mystery.[5] All of these unresearched variables introduces an important caveat for those concerned about negative effects on the environment. We simply cannot say "we know that wind energy is safe and environmentally friendly."

> *"All of these unresearched variables introduces an important caveat for those concerned about negative effects on the environment. We simply cannot say "we know that wind energy is safe and environmentally friendly."*

The seminar didn't mention all of these effects, but it did make clear that wind turbines make noise.

A big portion of the seminar dealt with the chronological order of the project. This was explained as follows.

First, the wind developer comes into an area (either invited or uninvited) to gather support. If successful, a small group of local investors is formed. Then, they each throw in maybe several thousand dollars to get things going. Next, they immediately start talking to farmers

---

[4] See chapter 9 for more on vibration and health concerns.
[5] It will likely stay a mystery as it will be particularly difficult to secure funds to research these areas—since they may ultimately demonstrate countless, unintended harmful effects of wind energy on the environment.

and landowners in the area trying to buy leases/easements to their property. Usually one of the local board members do this because a local face is more welcoming than a stranger.

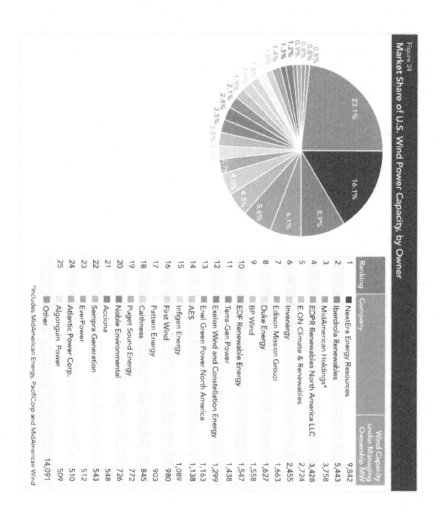

Figure 24
Market Share of U.S. Wind Power Capacity, by Owner

| Ranking | Company | Wind Capacity under Managing Ownership MW |
|---|---|---|
| 1 | NextEra Energy Resources | 9,842 |
| 2 | Iberdrola Renewables | 5,443 |
| 3 | MidAmerican Holdings* | 3,758 |
| 4 | EDPR Renewables North America LLC | 3,428 |
| 5 | E.ON Climate & Renewables | 2,724 |
| 6 | Invenergy | 2,455 |
| 7 | Edison Mission Group | 1,663 |
| 8 | Duke Energy | 1,627 |
| 9 | BP Wind | 1,558 |
| 10 | EDF Renewable Energy | 1,547 |
| 11 | Terra-Gen Power | 1,438 |
| 12 | Exelon Wind and Constellation Energy | 1,299 |
| 13 | Enel Green Power North America | 1,163 |
| 14 | AES | 1,138 |
| 15 | Infigen Energy | 1,089 |
| 16 | First Wind | 980 |
| 17 | Pattern Energy | 903 |
| 18 | Caithness | 845 |
| 19 | Puget Sound Energy | 772 |
| 20 | Noble Environmental | 726 |
| 21 | Acciona | 548 |
| 22 | Sempra Generation | 543 |
| 23 | EverPower | 512 |
| 24 | Atlantic Power Corp. | 510 |
| 25 | Algonquin Power | 509 |
| | Other | 14,091 |

*Includes MidAmerican Energy, PacifiCorp and MidAmerican Wind

After that, if the interest looks strong, the developer moves into county government to gain their favor. As the project moves forward even more, larger investors enter in to cover the biggest startup costs (towers may cost as much as $3 million each). When the whole "farm" is built—and many times before it's even finished—it is sold in its entirety to another investor or group of investors. These owners are typically foreign or multi-national corporations. The chart above from the American Wind Energy Association (statistics as of 2013) shows the market share of U.S. Wind Power Capacity by owner.

To get another angle on this situation, I produced my own table of owners by individually looking up each one (using Bloomberg, NASDAQ, etc.) and confirmed these findings from their own websites. I put the results in three categories: foreign owned, multinational (having wind projects anywhere outside of the US), and other/unknown.[6]

| Foreign | MWs | Multi-National | MWs | Other/Unknown | MWs |
|---------|-----|----------------|-----|---------------|-----|
| Iberdrola (Spain) | 5443 | Next Era Energy | 9842 | Mid American[7] | 3758 |
| EDPR (Spain) | 3428 | Invenergy | 2455 | Duke Energy | 1627 |
| E.ON (Germany) | 2724 | Edison Mission | 1663 | Terra Gen | 1438 |
| EDF (France) | 1547 | BP Wind[8] | 1558 | Exelon Wind | 1299 |
| ENEL (Italy) | 1163 | AES | 1138 | Caithness | 845 |
| Infigen (Australia)[9] | 1089 | First Wind[10] | 980 | Puget Sound | 772 |
| Acciona (Spain) | 548 | Pattern | 903 | Noble | 726 |
| Algonguin (Canada) | 509 | Sempra | 543 | Ever Power | 512 |
| | 0 | Atlantic Power | 510 | Other | 14091 |
| | 16451 | | 19592 | | 25068 |

What does all of this have to do with wind energy in South Dakota?

Everything. When combined with ownership information from the

---

[6] The unknown column was used for those entries that didn't fit the first two categories.

[7] Mid-American is Berkshire Hathaway (Warren Buffet).

[8] BP Wind is British Petroleum (60% foreign owned).

[9] Infigen is formerly Babcock and Brown.

[10] First Wind is a subsidiary of Sun Edison.

South Dakota PUC,[11] we come to realize that *ten out of the thirteen existing wind projects in South Dakota are already owned by foreign or multinational corporations.* These projects are listed below (the foreign and multi-nationally-owned companies are in **bold text**):

1. The South Dakota Wind Energy Center in Hyde County has 27 turbines that can produce 40.5 megawatts (MW) of energy. It is South Dakota's first major wind farm, beginning operation in 2003. It is owned by **NextEra Energy Resources** (formerly known as FPL Energy) and the power is sold to Basin Electric Power Cooperative.

2. The MinnDakota Wind Farm in Brookings County began operating its 36 turbines in January 2008. The farm can produce 54 MW of electricity. **Iberdrola Renewables** owns the wind farm and sells the electricity to Xcel Energy.

3. The Tatanka Wind Farm is located in McPherson County. Its 59 turbines began producing electricity in March 2008. It has a generating capacity of 88.5 MW. The project was developed by **Acciona Energy** and the power is sold into the MISO market.

4. The Wessington Springs Wind Project in Jerauld County began operating in February 2009. Owned by **Babcock & Brown**, the 51 MW of electricity the project is capable of producing with its 34 turbines is purchased by the Heartland Consumers Power District, which is headquartered in Madison, S.D.

5. Buffalo Ridge I Wind Farm, in Brookings County, is a 24-turbine farm capable of producing 50.4 MW of wind energy. Developed by **Iberdrola Renewables**, the wind farm began operation in April 2009. Northern Indiana Public Service Company purchases the power.

6. The first phase of the Titan Wind Project in Hand County went into production in December 2009. Built and operated by **BP Alternative Energy**, the energy from the 25-megawatt project is purchased by NorthWestern Energy. The wind farm has 10 turbines.

7. The Day County Wind Farm began operation in April 2010.It was developed by **NextEra Energy Resources** and features 66, 1.5-MW turbines. It has a generating capacity of 99 MW of energy, which is purchased by Basin Electric Power Cooperative.

---

[11] South Dakota Public Utilities Commission. "PUC Wind Handout." (November, 2016), 4. Accessed at http://puc.sd.gov/commission/energy/wind/pucwindhandout.pdf

8. Buffalo Ridge II Wind Farm in Brookings and Deuel counties has 105 turbines. The farm has a generating capacity of 210 MW of wind energy. Developer **Iberdrola Renewables** provides power to customers served by MISO. The wind farm began operation in December 2010.

9. The PrairieWinds SD1 Wind Project, located in Jerauld, Aurora and Brule counties, has 101, 1.5-MW turbines and has a generating capacity of 151.5 MW of wind energy. The project was developed by Basin Electric Power Cooperative and includes one turbine owned by Mitchell Technical Institute. The turbine is used in conjunction with MTI's Wind Turbine Technology Program. PrairieWinds SD1 began operation in February 2011 and the energy produced is also purchased by Basin Electric.

10. South Dakota Wind Partners Wind Project, located directly next to PrairieWinds SD1 wind farm in Jerauld County, consists of seven, 1.5-MW turbines. It has a generating capacity of 10.5 MW of wind energy. Like its neighboring project, Basin Electric Power Cooperative is also the developer and power purchaser of this project.

11. The Oak Tree Wind Farm, located in Clark County, began operations in December 2014. It has a total of 11 turbines with a combined capacity of 19.5 MW. Energy generated by the project, which is owned and operated by **Consolidated Edison Development**, is contracted to NorthWestern Energy.

12. The Beethoven Wind Farm, with a total capacity of 80 MW, is made up of 43 turbines located in Bon Homme, Hutchinson, and Charles Mix counties. The project came online in May 2015.

13. The Campbell County Wind Farm, developed by **Consolidated Edison Development**, began operation on Dec. 31, 2015. The 43-turbine project has a total capacity of approximately 94.3 MW and all generated power is purchased by Basin Electric Power Cooperative.

Smaller projects are located around Chamberlain, Howard, Gary, Canova, Carthage, Oaklane Colony and Rosebud. Altogether, South Dakota has more than 884 MW of wind energy installed. Other areas considered for wind energy development are the Coteau des Prairies in the northeast; Buffalo Ridge, which extends north-south from Marshall County to Brookings County; Turkey Ridge within Turner and Yankton counties; Fox Ridge near Faith; and several central South Dakota counties and tribal lands.

## Back to the Seminar

The instructor was neither pro-wind nor anti-wind. He just explained how it worked. But after this one-day lesson, it was clear to me that there would never be an industrial wind turbine on my property. Why not?

For the simple reason that it would ruin the land. It destroys the landscape, creates needless and intrusive noise, produces irritating shadow flicker over great distances, poses potential adverse health effects, and would *certainly* reduce the value of any building site and homes. One doesn't need to be a geophysicist, audiologist, or a real estate appraiser of rural properties to understand all of this.

Worst of all, basic property rights are compromised for up to *forty* years. Compromised by whom? *It is impossible to know.* The turbines and wind-rights are sold and resold in an endless cycle of musical-wind-investors. You—and later your heirs—ultimately become the landlord to a series of tenants that cannot be vetted. Chances are, they will consist of extremely powerful domestic or foreign corporations (quite possibly communist China) who may not have the landowner's best interest in mind.

And when the projects become technologically obsolete (if they haven't already), or if the owner goes broke, or if something simply goes wrong in the twenty, thirty, or forty years of operation, who is really responsible for taking down the monstrosity? What are the liabilities involved? The costs? These are serious risks that *no* landowner would ever entertain.

All of this was eye-opening. But at this point in the journey, I was still not educated on the real reason why investors and developers are so obsessed with the industry…

# — 2 —

# THE PRODUCTION TAX CREDIT

In 2014, the Midwestern billionaire Warren Buffet was quoted as saying:

> I will do anything that is basically covered by the law to reduce Berkshire's tax rate. For example, on wind energy, we get a tax credit if we build a lot of wind farms. That's the only reason to build them. They don't make sense without the tax credit.[12]

And that, friends, is why they build wind farms.

*Not* first and foremost for energy. *Not* first and foremost for saving the planet. Rather, wind projects are simply a means of redistributing a nation's tax money—siphoning off public funds to reduce the corporate taxes of a small, wealthy group.

In this chapter we'll unfold how this Production Tax Credit (PTC) actually works. This is important because wind energy cannot survive without the PTC. We will also look at how much wind energy receives from subsidies when compared to other forms of energy.

But before getting there, we should explore just why this federal support is necessary in the first place.

---

[12] Warren Buffet, cited in Nancy Pfotenhauer, "Big Wind's Bogus Subsidies: giving tax credits to the wind energy industry is a waste of time and money." *US News World and Report.* (May 12, 2014).
https://www.usnews.com/opinion/blogs/nancy-pfotenhauer/2014/05/12/even-warren-buffet-admits-wind-energy-is-a-bad-investment

## Wind: It's Not as Free as You Think

If wind energy is so great, why does it need to be subsidized?

In a word, because it is inherently *uninvestable*. The demand isn't there, and without the demand, there can be no profits, and without profits, there can be no investment. (Who wants to lose money?)

But this only pushes the economic question back another step: why is wind energy so uninvestable?

The answer is again very straightforward: because it's so *inefficient*. Many people are surprised to hear this because they're under the impression that "wind is free" and that the supply is "unlimited." There's some truth in this, but it's not that simple at all.

Gold in the ground, hydrogen from stars, and methane from cattle is also "free." But these things are only worth something to you and me if they can be feasibly collected, controlled, and distributed. Everyone faces *economic limitations*. We have to work within those limitations if any idea is going to succeed.

As it turns out, gold, hydrogen from space, and methane from cattle aren't very feasibly collected, controlled, and distributed. So they're expensive. The same goes for wind: it doesn't end up being feasible. We know this because it can't survive without subsidies (more on this in a moment). It's certainly not "unlimited," as there are plenty places on earth where the wind doesn't blow very hard, and other places on earth where it blows hard but not *consistently*, which is just as important.

The big problem is that wind isn't worth much in and of itself. It's not like other natural resources—food and water, that we depend on and use every day. Yes, I suppose we use wind for drying clothes in the summer or something similar. But it's not the most

> *"Wind has to be converted into something more useful, like electricity...this conversion process is very expensive and complicated."*

valuable commodity. Wind has to be *converted* into something more useful, like electricity.

The problem here is that this conversion process is *very* expensive and complicated. The logistical hurdles are endless. Let's look at just a few.

There's the electricity-storage obstacle mentioned earlier in the introduction. This is almost a game-stopper right off the bat. Commercial amounts of electricity cannot be stored in reserves like crude oil, nuclear materials, and firewood. The terminology of a wind "farm" breaks down at this point because there are no "bins" to store either the wind or the electricity month after month. ("Wind-farm" is therefore a *metaphor*, not a description.) Imagine trying to harvest corn at precisely the same time cattle need to be fed, and *only* at that time. It would be overwhelmingly complicated and inefficient!

Then there is the method of building, transporting, and constructing the turbines. This is costly and complex. The primary materials are steel and concrete—both heavy, and both expensive. The transportation method is truck and trailer across thousands of miles of the open Midwest. Three rigs won't even be sufficient to transport a single tower. And then there are miles and miles of copper wire for the grid—all of which needs to be buried underground in the right place and, sometimes, at the right time of year. All of this requires a labor force and a slew of highly-specialized tools and machinery (ironically, fueled by carbon-emitting gas and diesel).

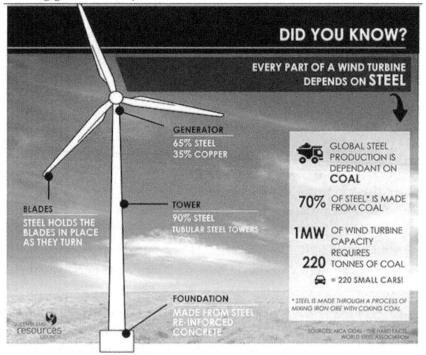

In addition to these difficulties, the general technology of "industrial wind turbines" is also primitive. They have endured virtually no technological or design upgrades in nearly a century. The basic design of a propeller-generator on a pole has been around for ages. Yes, a few modifications have been made to improve the existing model—better blade design and more efficient generators, but there's been little breakthroughs in new models altogether, certainly not for commercial use.[13]

## The Harmful Nature of Selective Subsidies

Of course, why would there be new breakthroughs in technology? *Because of subsidies,* there is no *need* to develop more efficient, more cost-effective, safer, cleaner forms of energy than the current technology. The government will support it

> *"Because of subsidies, there is no need to develop more efficient, more cost-effective, safer, cleaner forms of energy than the current technology."*

regardless of how inferior it is. The state can afford to lose money. Private investors can't. The government can raise taxes or print off dollar bills from the Federal Reserve Bank. Private investors can't do any of this (at least without going to prison). This is why any government-backed "investment" virtually always loses money.

Federal subsidies given toward energy *stifle* innovation. This is true for any government subsidy; the cash used to encourage certain projects *discourages* the goals people want. Welfare subsidizes poverty, incentivizing it through food stamps, housing, etc.; this makes poverty attractive and causes it to expand instead of shrink. Public schools that have poor graduation and literary rates are rewarded with more federal funds, expanding substandard education even more. The same goes for healthcare and a dozen other federal programs. (If throwing cash at a

---

[13] Out of the six new wind turbine designs featured in an *Engadget* article, three don't have blades and boast other superior features over traditional industrial turbines. See Cat DiStasio, "Six New Wind Turbine Designs." *Engadget* (November 5, 2016). Because of federal funding, developers have little incentive to use—or even pay attention to—these new designs.

problem would fix it, the world's problems would have been fixed a long time ago!) When it comes to business, capitalism punishes losers and rewards winners, but crony-capitalism does the opposite: it punishes the *winners* and rewards the *losers*.[14]

In the same way, subsidizing inefficient forms of energy encourages precisely that: inefficient forms of energy. Wind energy is an economic loser. If it wasn't, it could survive without federal help.

All of this means that if a person or political administration is truly "pro-wind," they would *stop enabling* developers to mass-produce inferior, inefficient, unsustainable, wasteful forms of energy—so wasteful, in fact, that the wind projects go bankrupt

> *"Wind energy is an economic loser. If it wasn't, it could survive without federal help."*

even while being fed cash from the government.[15] Here is a sample of popular headlines from just the last two years:

LUVERNE — The 360 investors in a rural Rock County wind energy company stand to lose thousands of dollars after MinWind Energy, LLC., filed for Chapter 11 bankruptcy last week in Minnesota Bankruptcy Court.[16]

NEW YORK — SunEdison, a one-time star in the alternative energy field, is filing for bankruptcy protection after years of rapid-fire acquisitions left the solar company in a desperate cash situation. The company, which has permits for five wind farm projects in Maine, filed with the Bankruptcy Court for the Southern District of New York on Thursday.[17]

---

[14] See Henry Hazlitt, *Economics in One Lesson* (Auburn: Von Mises Institute, 2008) and Thomas DiLorenzo, *The Problem With Socialism* (Washington D.C.: Regnery, 2016).

[15] This isn't even to mention the dangers and unreliability of the turbines—as manifested in their collapse, catching fire, and extremely costly maintenance. Case studies here are too numerous to survey. Even the confidentiality clauses of the wind-rights contracts can't conceal many of these deadly incidents (which have occasionally been covered by the media).

[16] Julie Bantjer, "MinWind Files for Bankruptcy," *The Globe* (Jan 14, 2015).

[17] Maine wind power developer SunEdison files for bankruptcy protection," *Portland Press Herald* (April 21, 2016).

Noble Environmental Power LLC, a wind-energy company backed by billionaire Michael Dell, filed for bankruptcy protection on Thursday in a debt-for-equity restructuring deal.[18]

A 2015 study conducted by FTI Consulting concluded that roughly 25% of wind companies go under. "The wind industry saw more than 120 suppliers have been 'burned' in the past 24 months, of which 88 from Asia, 23 from Europe, and 18 from North Americas."[19] The legal mess falling out from these events is happening as I write these words, and it isn't pretty.[20]

Pro-wind groups should respect the laws of economics instead of trying to challenge them. Allow supply and demand to work so that the free-market and its entrepreneurs can create better forms of energy.[21] This is how all wealth, goods, and services are produced in the first place: by private innovation, not by kingly decree.

You can see, then, why it is so unfortunate that wind energy receives the *most* tax-payer subsidies of all other forms of energy (see chart below). When the pro-wind crowd hears about subsidies, they often respond by saying, "But fossil fuels receive subsidies, too." This is true—but misleading. The second chart below puts the fossil fuel subsidy vs. the wind and solar subsidy into perspective by comparing the subsidy to how

---

[18] Sarah Chaney, "Michael Dell-Backed Noble Environmental Files for Bankruptcy," *Wall Street Journal* (September 15, 2016).

[19] FTI Consulting, "Global Wind Supply Chain Update 2015," http://www.fticonsulting.com/fti-intelligence/energy/research/clean-energy/global-wind-supply-chain-update-2015

[20] See for example, Mark Del Franco, "Small Project In Illinois Could Make Big Headlines In Wind Farm Construction," *North American Wind Power* (June 23, 2015). This case involved foreclosure on a wind farm and complicated rulings about whether the towers qualify as "real property" or "personal property." The article says, "GSG 7, the landowners and Clipper filed motions to throw out AUI's lien claim on a number of grounds. One of those grounds was that the 300-foot post-ensioned concrete tower and foundation that AUI built was a trade fixture that is not 'lienable' under Illinois law. The court agreed with that argument and ruled against AUI."

[21] A perfect example is the invention of the "Vortex turbine," a bladeless and more environmentally-friendly turbine design from Spain that was privately supported by a crowdfunding campaign in 2015 (see vortexbladeless.com). This makes us ask: if current technology is so "green," why are private individuals willing to spend so much of their own time and energy to produce a different design?

much electricity is generated.[22] Fossil fuels currently generate roughly 67% of the electricity in the U.S., and wind less than 5%.[23] The facts speak for themselves!

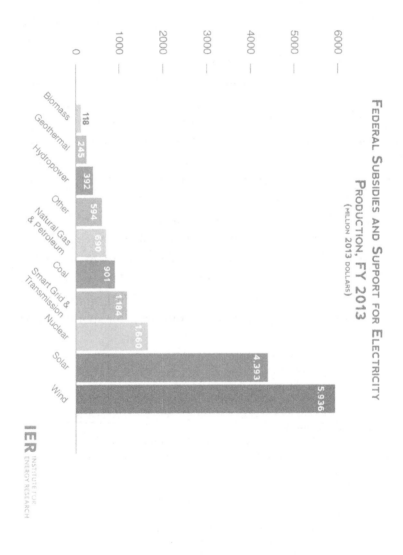

---

[22] The two charts below come from The Institute for Energy Research. Cf. Mary Hutzler, "Subsidizing American Energy: A Breakdown By Source." *The Institute for Energy Research.* http://instituteforenergyresearch.org/studies/energy-subsidies-study/
[23] For reasons already mentioned above, I would be in favor of eliminating *all* energy subsidies

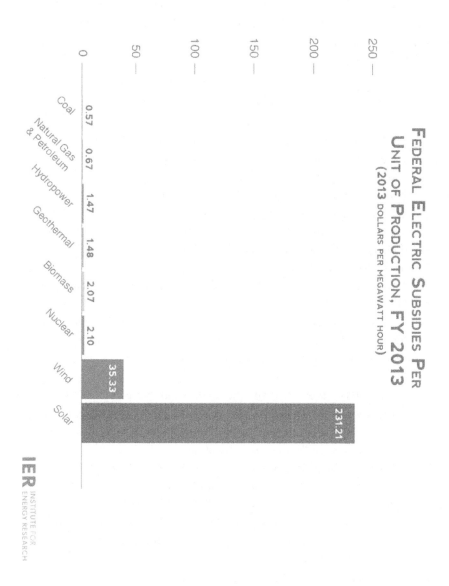

FEDERAL ELECTRIC SUBSIDIES PER
UNIT OF PRODUCTION, FY 2013
(2013 DOLLARS PER MEGAWATT HOUR)

| | |
|---|---|
| Coal | 0.57 |
| Natural Gas & Petroleum | 0.67 |
| Hydropower | 1.47 |
| Geothermal | 1.48 |
| Biomass | 2.07 |
| Nuclear | 2.10 |
| Wind | 35.33 |
| Solar | 231.21 |

IER
INSTITUTE FOR
ENERGY RESEARCH

## The Production Tax Credit

Wind "farms" are so inefficient that direct subsidies aren't even enough to make it investable. What's offered instead is something more personal. It's something every wealthy individual hunts for…

A tax deduction.

Here's the history of the "Production Tax Credit" (PTC) from the American Wind Energy Association website itself:

> Sen. Chuck Grassley (R-IA) originally authored the PTC. It was enacted as part of the Energy Policy Act of 1992, helping launch the wind industry as we know it. The first lapse of the credit occurred seven years later in 1999, causing a near halt in production. Since then, Congress cycled through the tax credit in one or two-year stints, and allowed it to expire multiple times. This cyclical pattern resulted in boom-bust cycles of development. The PTC phasedown agreed to in December 2015 was thanks to strong bipartisan support, supplying much-needed policy certainty. The PTC and ITC has driven more wind development— especially as utilities, Fortune 500 companies and municipalities seek more low-cost, clean renewable energy. The tax credits, extended through 2019, have begun phasing down by 20 percent each year beginning in 2017. Here are the legislation's details:

> For the PTC (Sec. 301 of the bill), wind projects that started construction in 2015 and 2016 receive a full value PTC of 2.3 cents per kilowatt hour. For projects that begin construction in 2017, the credit is at 80 percent of full value; in 2018, 60 percent PTC; and in 2019, 40 percent PTC. Similarly, for the ITC election for wind energy (Sec. 302 of the bill), projects that started construction in 2015 and 2016 are eligible for a full 30 percent ITC; for 2017, a 24 percent ITC; for 2018, an 18 percent ITC; and in 2019, a 12 percent ITC. As before, the rules will allow wind projects to qualify as long as they start construction before the end of the period.[24]

The Production Tax Credit (PTC) is not a direct payment. It is a *tax* credit. Say your tax bill for the year is $10 million dollars. If you own

---

[24] AWEA. "Production Tax Credit." http://www.awea.org/production-tax-credit

enough wind turbines, your tax bill could shrink to *zero*.

How many wind turbines would that take? It depends. But here is the general rule of thumb that a South Dakota PUC staff member told me:

> You can expect a wind tower to achieve an approximate 40% capacity factor. That is, it will be able to put out about 40% of its potential. With that assumption, the calculation would look like this:
>
> 1.85 MW x 8760 hours/year = 16,206 MWh annual potential
>
> 16,206 MWh x 40% capacity factor = 6,482.4 MWh estimated annual generation from 1 turbine
>
> 6,482.4 MWh x 1,000 kWh/MWh x $.023/kWh = $149,095.20 Production Tax Credit per turbine per year for the first 10 years.

You can see, then, why after the projects are built they are *sold* to somebody with a huge (or as Trump would say, *Yuge!*) income tax liability. In the Beethoven Wind project ten miles north of my house, there are forty-three towers. They have 1.85 MW capacity each. The estimated tax credit on that wind farm is $6,400,000 per year, or for the full ten years it is $64 million dollars. Warren Buffet was right.

What happens when the tax credit goes away? You already heard from the quote above from the AWEA. But let's visualize this problem as well[25]:

---

[25] Richard Caperton, "Good Government Investments in Renewable Energy." *Center for American Progress* (January 10, 2012).
https://www.americanprogress.org/issues/green/reports/2012/01/10/10956/good-government-investments-in-renewable-energy/

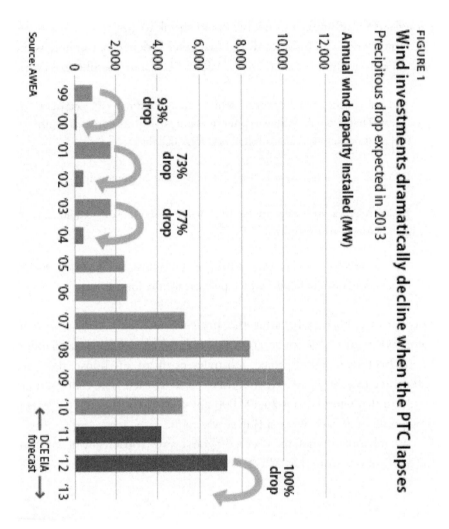

**FIGURE 1**

**Wind investments dramatically decline when the PTC lapses**

Precipitous drop expected in 2013

Annual wind capacity installed (MW)

Source: AWEA

This confirms Warren Buffet's statement yet again. Remember, his statement was not "The production tax credit is a *good reason* to build wind farms," or "The production tax credit is *one of many reasons* to build wind farms." His statement was, "That's the *only* reason to build them. They don't make sense without the tax credit" (emphasis mine).

Once a person finally wraps their head around this reality, it becomes much more clear why wind energy in the U.S. really is a "scam."

## Crony-Capitalism at Its Best

I'm not the only one to make this observation. I want to conclude the chapter with extended excerpts of a short article from the *National Review*. Robert Bryce, a Senior Fellow at the Manhattan Institute, probes the inner workings of the wind-farm crony-capitalist project.

It takes enormous amounts of taxpayer cash to make wind energy seem affordable. Last month, during its annual conference, the American Wind Energy Association issued a press release trumpeting the growth of wind-energy capacity. It quoted the association's CEO, Tom Kiernan, who declared that the wind business is "an American success story." There's no doubt that wind-energy capacity has grown substantially in recent years. But that growth has been fueled not by consumer demand, but by billions of dollars' worth of taxpayer money. According to data from Subsidy Tracker, a database maintained by Good Jobs First, a Washington, D.C. based organization that promotes "corporate and government accountability in economic development and smart growth for working families", the total value of the subsidies given to the biggest players in the U.S. wind industry is now $176 billion.

That sum includes all local, state, and federal subsidies as well as federal loans and loan guarantees received by companies on the American Wind Energy Association's board of directors since 2000. (Most of the federal grants have been awarded since 2007.) Of the $176 billion provided to the wind-energy sector, $2.9 billion came from local and state governments; $9.4 billion came from federal grants and tax credits; and $163.9 billion was provided in the form of federal loans or loan guarantees.

General Electric—the biggest wind-turbine maker in North America—has a seat on AWEA's board. It has received $1.6 billion in local, state, and federal subsidies and $159 billion in federal loans and loan guarantees. (It's worth noting that General Electric got into the wind business in 2002 after it bought Enron Wind, a company that helped pioneer the art of renewable-energy rent-seeking.)

NextEra Energy, the largest wind-energy producer in the U.S., has received about 50 grants and tax credits from local, state, and federal entities as well as federal loans and loan guarantees worth $5.5 billion...

About $6.8 billion in subsidies, loans, and loan guarantees went to foreign corporations, including Iberdrola, Siemens, and E.On. Those three companies, and five other foreign companies, have seats on AWEA's board of directors.

Many of the companies on the AWEA board will be collecting even more federal subsidies over the next few years. In December, the Congressional Joint Committee on Taxation estimated that the latest renewal of the production tax credit will cost U.S. taxpayers about $3.1 billion per year from now until 2019. That subsidy pays wind-energy companies $23 for each megawatt-hour of electricity they produce.

That's an astounding level of subsidy. In 2014 and 2015, according to the Energy Information Administration, during times of peak demand, the average wholesale price of electricity was about $50 per megawatt-hour. Last winter in Texas, peak wholesale electricity prices averaged $21 per megawatt hour. Thus, on the national level, wind-energy subsidies are worth nearly half the cost of wholesale power, and in the Texas market, those subsidies can actually exceed the wholesale price of electricity.

Of course, wind-energy boosters like to claim that the oil-and-gas sector gets favorable tax treatment, too. That may be so, but those tax advantages are tiny when compared with the federal gravy being ladled on wind companies. Recall that the production tax credit is $23 per megawatt-hour. A megawatt-hour of electricity contains 3.4 million Btu. That means wind-energy producers are getting a subsidy of $6.76 per million Btu. The current spot price of natural gas is about $2.40 per million Btu. Thus, on an energy-equivalent basis, wind energy's subsidy is nearly three times the current market price of natural gas.

MidAmerican Energy Company, a subsidiary of Berkshire Hathaway, has a seat on AWEA's board. Berkshire's subsidy total: $1.5 billion—and it's primed to collect lots more. In April, the company announced plans to spend $3.6 billion on wind projects in Iowa…

Keep in mind that the $176 billion figure in wind-energy subsidies is a minimum number. It counts only subsidies given to companies on AWEA's board. Not counted are subsidies handed out to companies like Google, which got part of a $490 million federal cash grant for investing in an Oregon wind project. Nor does it include the $1.5 billion in subsidies given to SunEdison, the now-bankrupt company that used to have a seat on AWEA's board. (To download the full list of subsidies garnered by AWEA's board members, click here.)

Nor does that figure include federal money given to J. P. Morgan and Bank of America, both of which have a seat on AWEA's board.

The two banks received federal loans or loan guarantees worth $1.29 trillion and $3.49 trillion, respectively. In an e-mail, Phil Mattera, the research director for Good Jobs First, told me that the loan and loan-guarantee figures for the banks include the federal bailout package known as the Troubled Asset Relief Program as well as "programs instituted by the Federal Reserve in the wake of the financial meltdown." When all of the subsidies, loans, and loan guarantees given to the companies on AWEA's board are counted, the grand total comes to a staggering $5.1 trillion.

According to Wikipedia, crony capitalism "may be exhibited by favoritism in the distribution of legal permits, government grants, special tax breaks, or other forms of state interventionism." Wind-energy companies are getting favoritism on every count. The U.S. Fish and Wildlife Service wants to give those companies permits allowing them to legally kill bald and golden eagles with their turbines for up to 30 years. The industry is getting grants, tax breaks, and loans worth billions. And thanks to federal mandates like the Clean Power Plan and state renewable-energy requirements—nearly all of which are predicated on the specious claim that paving vast swaths of the countryside with wind turbines is going to save us from catastrophic climate change—the industry is surfing a wave of state interventionism.

AWEA's Kiernan likely has it right. In a country where having a profitable business increasingly requires getting favors from government, the U.S. wind industry is definitely a "success."[26]

---

[26] Robert Bryce, "Wind-Energy Sector Gets $176 Billion Worth of Crony Capitalism." *National Review* (June 6, 2016).

# — 3 —

# PURPA

Unmerited, privileged status[27] has been conferred to wind energy in even more ways than subsidies and the Production Tax Credit. But here, our tale leaves the halls of congress and leather chairs of corporate board-rooms and into the bloody deserts of Palestine.

### The Oil Crisis and Western Response

It was Jerusalem on October 6, 1973. Millions of Jews were celebrating the most holy day on their calendar, the "Day of Atonement." But events took an unexpected turn. Syria and Egypt attacked Israel as part of the ongoing, 20th-century Palestinian-Israeli conflict. The U. S. government ultimately supported Israel in the effort. In response, the Organization of Arab Petroleum Exporting Countries (OAPEC) proclaimed an oil embargo. Because these countries had a near monopoly on the world's production of oil, prices skyrocketed from $3/barrel to a whopping $11/barrel in just one year.

The American economy was crushed from these high prices. It became clear that America was far too "dependent on foreign oil"—a phrase that become house-hold economic vocabulary ever since. So, the federal government stepped in to "fix things."

Congress passed the National Energy Act of 1978, which included

---

[27] See Matthew Mitchell, *The Pathology of Privilege: The Economic Consequences of Government Favoritism* (Fairfax: Mercatus Center, 2015).

five major statutes designed to control supply and demand of energy in case an embargo like this one (or some other event) would ever occur again. The idea was to promote energy conservation, energy efficiency, and renewable methods of fuel. How? Through the only way the government can: forcing funds out of the citizenry and redistributing them to enact subsidies, tax credits, and regulation.

One of the most substantial of these five statutes was the Public Utility Regulatory Practices Act (PURPA). It aimed at growing hydro-electric power, conserving electricity and natural gas, and adjusted pricing methods in public utilities. In the words of the Federal Energy Regulatory Commission, PURPA's purposes are:

1. The conservation of electric energy,
2. Increased efficiency in the use of facilities and resources by electric utilities,
3. Equitable retail rates for electric consumers,
4. Expeditious development of hydroelectric potential at existing small dams, and
5. Conservation of natural gas while ensuring that rates to natural gas consumers are equitable.

In effect, PURPA came to socialize major aspects of the energy industry.

### PURPA: A Blessing...or a Curse?

Through these changes, PURPA created a new class of power-producers called "Qualifying Facilities," which receive special discounts and privileges. These qualifying facilities are either "small power production" facilities (wind/solar, usually less than 80MW or 20MW capacity) or "cogenerational" (a plant that produces both electricity and some other form of energy more efficiently than if produced separately). For the first category, wind and solar-based producers have been fighting over this coveted status ever since the policies came into effect in the late 1970s and early 1980s.

How does one "qualify" to be a "qualifying facility"? The major factor for wind energy is in not building a wind farm over a certain megawatt capacity. But of course, developers work around this threshold by breaking up their large projects into smaller ones. This has been recently noted:

> On June 29, 2016, FERC heard input from utilities, grid operators, small power producers and cogenerators to determine if the current regime works under contemporary market structures. Utilities spoke of the need to overhaul PURPA due to the unsustainably high prices they are obligated to pay renewables development. Developers insisted that these purchase obligations provide the certainty needed to refund the cost of building these small solar and wind facilities. Additionally, FERC heard testimony regarding small producers "gaming the system" by deliberately staying under the 20 MW threshold at a particular site but building strings of 20 MW installations far enough apart to be considered separate entities—effectively creating utility-scale projects that are not regulated as utilities. The review also considered the role of tax incentives and Renewable Portfolio Standards (RPS).[28]

As also alluded to in the quote above, the big kicker about PURPA is that it requires investor-owned utilities to buy power produced by Qualifying Facilities.[29] This complicates the energy market significantly.

Wind developers want to stay profitable, but to do so, they have to be ensured that someone is going to buy their electricity. This conflicts with the utility company's own interest to profit by buying affordable electricity that they can sell to consumers. Like any socialist price-controlling scheme, a host of problems are created down each link in the chain of buyers and sellers. None of this would ever occur if electricity was treated

---

[28] John Kirkwood and Andrew Wheeler, "FERC Weighs PURPA Changes: What Do Renewable Energy Stakeholders Need to Know?" *Faegre Baker Daniels* (August 22, 2016). https://www.faegrebd.com/ferc-weighs-purpa-changes-what-do-renewable-energy-stakeholders-need

[29] "The Energy Policy Act of 2005, however, created an important exception that, in short, has resulted in FERC removing a utility's mandatory purchase requirement for most QFs over 20 MWs located in independent system operator and regional transmission organization regions.[4] This exception is based on the theory that these QFs are presumed to have nondiscriminatory access to day-ahead and real-time energy markets and wholesale markets for long-term sales of capacity and energy. QFs in this category with unique operating characteristics or transmission constraints, however, can try to get FERC to override this exception." Daniel Simon, "Understanding PURPA Rights In Power Purchase Agreements." *Law360* (August 28, 2015).

like any other good/service on the market—where supply and demand determine prices, and people make purchases voluntarily.

The demand for electricity fluctuates both throughout the day and throughout various times of year. Utility companies employ dozens of energy traders to secure enough power to go around. But by forcing companies to buy electricity from wind, they may end up buying electricity that they don't actually want or need—and buying it for a price that they don't want or can't afford.

One article tries to explain all of these complicated contingencies:

> …a utility is not always a particularly willing buyer when executing a PURPA PPA. As a result, a utility may propose a PURPA PPA with terms and conditions that are more onerous to the QF developer than those in a non-PURPA PPA. Because FERC's regulations provide that, once a PPA is executed and effective, the QF may be viewed to have waived certain rights, it is critical that a QF developer know and understand its PURPA rights prior to executing a PPA.

> First, FERC requires a utility to purchase all scheduled and unscheduled energy delivered by a QF. Therefore, when a utility provides a PURPA PPA with scheduling requirements, the QF should be sure before executing the PPA that the provisions will not result in a QF failing to receive payment for unscheduled energy it delivers. Scheduling restrictions can become particularly important for intermittent resources, such as wind and solar, that raise unique scheduling challenges.

> Second, FERC's regulations strictly limit a utility's ability to curtail energy delivered by a QF, and therefore not pay for the energy it would have otherwise received.[30]

---

[30] Simon, "Understanding PURPA's Rights."

It's a mess for sure.

But you can see why PURPA would make the qualifying facilities (like wind developers) so happy: the government threatens utility companies that don't buy their electricity! Imagine if this happened in any other business situation—where an entrepreneur had to *threaten* people to buy their products. This is a strong indicator that wind energy isn't ready for the marketplace; it's not producing something that others are actually *willing* to buy.

> *"Imagine if...an entrepreneur had to threaten people to buy their products. This is a strong indicator that wind energy isn't ready for the marketplace..."*

Utility companies have rightly objected to this mandated purchasing. Note the following comments from a 2016 letter submitted to Federal Energy Regulatory Commission by Duke Energy (Carolinas), the largest PURPA project energy provider in the United States:

> As PURPA purchases are mandated regardless of need, they displace existing useful and operating capacity assets that already are in consumer rates. It is, therefore, neither equitable to customers nor in the public interest for customers to be burdened with the costs of new purchases when no needs are being avoided, in addition to also bearing the costs of existing useful assets.[31]

Not only is it unfair, but PURPA's mandated-purchases result in a more unreliable power grid:

> Congress intended for PURPA to conserve energy and improve – not impair – system reliability, but those goals cannot be and are not being achieved by a must-take mandatory purchase obligation...An obligation to purchase in excess of load needs, unconstrained deployment of high levels of must-take QF generation much of which cannot be reliably forecasted, combined with

---

[31] Kendall Bowman of Duke Energy, letter submitted to Kimberly Bose (June 7, 2016). Available at
https://www.ferc.gov/CalendarFiles/20160617152411-
Bowman,%20Duke%20Energy%20-%20Long%20paper.pdf

no requirements on QFs to contribute to or support parallel and reliable system operations, encourages imprudent siting and operational practices by QFs, which impair the utility's ability to balance load to generation and prudently manage operational reliability.[32]

This was confirmed by an MIT study done regarding wind energy in Texas:

"Texas is learning just how costly it is to wrangle the wind," MIT researchers found. Texas is already spending $8 billion, but the state's utilities and transmission companies will have to spend hundreds of millions more to upgrade the system enough to transport electricity from wind-rich West Texas to market in East Texas, the report found. Texas' new wind turbines also place dangerous stress on the power grid, potentially leading to blackouts.

"Wind power suffers from two fatal flaws: unfortunate geography and unreliable output," Travis Fisher, an economist at the Institute for Energy Research, told The Daily Caller News Foundation.[33]

The result of all of this is paradoxical, but undeniable: *higher electricity costs.* (More on this in coming chapters).

It seems, then, the PURPA is another failing experiment in controlling an economy. Coercion and central planning creates economic chaos.

### PURPA in South Dakota, Montana, and Idaho

The Beethoven Wind Farm in South Dakota used PURPA to force Northwestern Energy to buy their electricity. The "Farm" has a general capacity of 79.55 MW—just under the 80MW PURPA threshold for that project. In late 2016, I witnessed Prevailing Winds break up their project from a 200 MW project to 13 projects, all less than 20MW, again to qualify for PURPA. They filed these thirteen applications with the South Dakota PUC in December of 2016—despite promising not to do this very thing months earlier.

---

[32] Ibid.
[33] Andrew Follett, "Costly Wind Turbines Are Damaging Texas Power Grid, MIT Study Finds." *The Daily Caller* (August 8, 2016).

Montana's Public Service Commission has temporarily suspended guaranteed rates for small solar projects at the request of NorthWestern Energy. Commissioner Roger Koopman, who voted in favor of the suspension, said solar developers are streaming into Montana to take advantage of the high rates. "They look at Montana and they kind of flood in here thinking we can cut a really fat hog with this $66 rate," he commented on Montana Public Radio, "which is totally unfair to the rate payer and totally unfair to Montana businesses, totally unfair to Montana industries."[34]

The Idaho Public Utilities Commission recently granted a request made by the state's major utilities to reduce the length of negotiated renewable energy contracts covered by PURPA.[35] The decision reduces the length of contracts to two years, after regulators found longer contracts led to customers paying higher costs for renewable power.

In conclusion, PURPA is truly a poor piece of legislation that is currently being gamed by wind and solar developers. Developers size their projects to get a guaranteed rate for the electricity for a long term (up to 20 years). All of this ends up costing the consumer more money, encourages wasteful business practices, builds a less reliable power grid, and distorts energy prices in the economy.

---

[34] Quote in Peter Maloney, "Montana Suspends PURPA rates for small solar farms." *UtilityDive* (June 20, 2016). http://www.utilitydive.com/news/montana-psc-suspends-purpa-rates-for-small-solar-farms/421151/
[35] Ibid.

# — 4 —

# The American Wind Energy Association

The American Wind Energy Association is the central lobbying group for the American wind industry. According to its website (awea.org), wind energy is the "fastest growing energy industry" and is a "clean source of electricity for American consumers." Its stated agenda is:

Driving demand for more wind energy
Making wind energy as cost-competitive as possible
Implementing policies that help with deployment and operations
Building the political strength we need to implement our agenda

Generous and smooth—like any lobbyist organization should sound.

But if you accept the premise that the wind industry cannot survive without the Production Tax Credit, and that the goal is to build "the political strength we need to implement our agenda," then you will want to start "following the money."

### Follow the Money!

According to opensecrets.org, from the election cycles between 2011-2016, our South Dakota Senator Mike Rounds received $24,800 from Berkshire Hathaway and $18,750 from NextEra Energy. Senator John

Thune received $52,000 from NextEra Energy and Representative Kristi Noem received $10,000 from NextEra Energy. In addition, Chuck Grassley, who first proposed the PTC back in 1992, received $29,500 from NextEra and $21,150 from Renewable Energy Group.[36]

A quick internet search revealed these contributions and it is sufficient to show that that wind energy is no different than any other crony-capitalist scheme. The industry pays off lobbyists and congressmen to vote for the pro-wind agenda; laws and regulations are put in place that give an unfair advantage (e.g., tax credits) to a select group in (an otherwise) free market. The mass of taxpayers pay for the credits given to these select corporations.[37]

In other words, the larger middle class is robbed for the benefit of the small and elite wealthy—all in the name of "jobs" and "saving the earth."

> *"The larger middle-class is robbed for the benefit of the small and elite wealthy—all in the name of "jobs" and "saving the earth."*

(And then the same politicians pretend to care about a "shrinking middle-class"!) If time allowed, one could probably dig through campaign finance money that's been going to these same individuals ever since they first set foot in D. C. And this is just *four* of five-hundred and thirty-five congressmen.

This is sickening. In the last couple years, I have personally sent letter upon letter to my three "representatives" in Washington. All that I've ever received was a form letter telling me of their support for "all of the sources of energy." This is nonsense, because energy sectors are in *competition*. Saying "I'm for all energy" is like saying "I'm for all football teams; I want everyone to win." This is meaningless.

---

[36] NextEra has a subsidiary called NextEra Energy Resources, LLC, which "together with its affiliated entities, is the world's largest generator of renewable energy from the wind and sun." See nexteraenergyresources.com. These figures represent campaign donations. The amount of cash politicians receive from various crony-capitalists "off the record" is always an unknown, but probably remains substantial.

[37] The AWEA reports that wind energy produced 4.7% of the electricity generated in the United States in 2015. Additionally, the production tax credit given to developers, investors and owners was $128 billion dollars. See AWEA, "U.S. number one in the world in wind energy production" (February 26, 2016).
http://www.awea.org/MediaCenter/pressrelease.aspx?ItemNumber=8463

## Wind Energy and the Climate Change Narrative

"The urge to save humanity is almost always a false front for the urge to rule."
—H. L. Mencken

No human project, plan, or effort can make sense without a larger story. This is true whether the stories prove to be truthful or not.

Wind energy is given life-saving significance by being placed in the context of the global-warming (or "climate change") narrative. The AWEA *Siting Handbook* makes this clear:

> *"Wind energy is given life-saving significance by being placed in the context of the global-warming narrative."*

Global warming is considered one of the most serious problems facing the global community. Certain gases, such as carbon dioxide, when released in the atmosphere through the burning of fossil fuels, create a "greenhouse effect." Clean, renewable energy solutions, such as wind, solar, and hydroelectric systems, that do not rely on fossil fuels for energy generation help curb the effects of global warming. Throughout the United States, many local and state governments have set mandates or passed laws to encourage clean energy generation by requiring utilities to produce a portion of electricity from renewable sources. Although wind has been used as an energy source for centuries, only within the last 30 years have advances in technology allowed wind energy to become an increasingly important part of the nation's energy mix. Since 1974 the American Wind Energy Association (AWEA) has been committed to encouraging and assisting wind energy development in the United States.[38]

The *urgency* of the climate-change story is used as an excuse to force wind-produced electricity down the throats of utility companies and consumers. "If we wait for the market to innovate better forms of energy, there may not be enough time," we're told. "The ends justifies the means; we must use force to save ourselves from the catastrophe that awaits all

---

[38] Aileen Giovanello (Tetra Tech EC) and Carolyn Kaplan (Nixon Peabody LLP), *Wind Energy Siting Handbook* (Washington D.C.: The American Wind Energy Association, 2008), 183.

humanity."[39] We then have the carbon tax, mandated-electricity purchases, countless "carbon offset" fees, and more and more threats from the government.

Fortunately, this alarmism doesn't add up. First of all, it makes no sense to argue that federal policies can save the world. There is nothing more slow and incompetent than politicians who are primarily concerned about their

> *"To leave the task of engineering the world's most 'green' energy to a committee in Washington D. C. will only secure our fate, not stop it."*

own re-election, and that's what the federal government is comprised of. To leave the task of engineering the world's most "green" energy to a committee in Washington D. C. will only *secure* our fate, not stop it. As it's been said, there is nothing more permanent than a temporary government program, nothing more hopeless than an optimistic politician, and nothing more short-sighted than central "planners." These ironies haunt our lives every election cycle.

Second of all, there are serious doubts about whether the grand narrative of climate change is even accurate—or to what extent it is.[40] This is partly due to the computer modeling required to make future, theoretical projections. Models are *models*, not reality. "The map is not the territory," as the saying goes. I'm not a climatologist, atmospheric scientist, or geophysicist, but my own opinion is that climate change is blown way out of proportion and may even be a political hoax altogether.

Whether that's the case or not, nobody likes pollution. We've all seen the photos of the smog in China and are glad that we live somewhere else. It makes a person think: what if some of the money spent on taxpayer subsidies for wind would have been put to use in research and development of genuinely clean and green energy, whether coal, natural gas, nuclear, or otherwise? Surely this would be a wiser "investment."

---

[39] This is also a way for scientists to secure their research funding. As one biologist remarked, "Scientists have realized that frightening the public brings in dollars." Sylvan Wittwer, cited in Richard Stroup, *Eco-Nomics* (Washington D.C.: Cato Institute, 2003), 84.
[40] See Donald C. Morton, "Will a return of rising temperatures validate the climate models?" *Climate Etc.* (December 15, 2014); Alan Moron, ed., *Climate Change* (Woodsville: Stockade Books, 2015); James Delingpole, "Global Warming is myth—so say 80 graphs from 58 peer-reviewed scientific papers published in 2017." *Breitbart* (June 6, 2017).

## The AWEA Developer's Playbook

The social and political strategy of the AWEA can also be found in the *Siting Handbook*. The portions below reveal the shrewd methods necessary to successfully colonize an area:

Planning public outreach is a crucial aspect of the siting process and should be commenced in the initial planning stages. This section discusses the role of the developer in communicating with various audiences, how to convey a message, and when and where to conduct public outreach activities. "Know your audience" is the key to any phase of siting and permitting. Whether the developer is facing a regulator, a neighborhood, or the media, it is important to communicate effectively with those interested in the project. The most successful wind energy projects are those in which all stakeholders feel a sense of ownership and empowerment. The challenge is to promote this inclusiveness to gain allies without losing control over the process and the developer's message. During the siting process, the developer will get to know the local, regional, and state political issues and players. The developer may pick a spokesperson who is knowledgeable about the details of the proposed project and who will be available to answer questions. Some developers find it helpful to consult with a public relations specialist to create a public outreach plan and schedule. Factors to be weighed in deciding whether or not to hire such a consultant include the location, complexity, and schedule of the proposed project, as well as any particular concerns about wind energy projects or positions held by regulators and permitting authorities, the community, abutters, and the media. The developer should forge positive relationships with government officials. Public officials usually want to know about proposed developments before the general public. Public officials often can alert the developer to more obscure obstacles or concerns that might be addressed before the project is announced. Minor project adjustments may be made in response to concerns voiced by public officials. Although officials may not agree with every aspect of the project, gaining their respect through proactive communication is worthwhile. The developer should explain how the project will promote the positive impacts of wind power, such as energy generation with no air or water pollution, utilization of domestic sources of energy rather than reliance on foreign imports, increased energy security and independence, benefits for the municipality including an increased tax base and modest increases in local jobs, and creation of a potential tourist attraction. The socioeconomics discussion in Section 5.7 provides additional information regarding increased tax base and local job creation. Many local officials want to be identified with local development projects and can become valuable allies in presenting the project to the community. It is usually easiest to develop such relationships with local officials, although the developer should approach state and federal officials as well. The developer may coordinate with government officials early in the process to communicate with the public during the development of a proposed project. After local officials and regulators have been briefed on the project, the developer might offer to meet with neighborhood and community leaders. The best way for people to hear about a project is directly from the developer, before any opposition can spread misinformation about the project and its potential impacts. The developer may consider distributing leaflets in an area or sending bulk mailings from the local post office. Once the community knows the developer's plans, the developer may consider consulting with neighbors and abutters to give them an opportunity to comment before formal proposals are submitted for review by regulators or permitting agencies.[41]

After reading all of this manipulative verbiage, one gets the idea that the AWEA has a political agenda to get the local governmental officials on their side "before any opposition can spread misinformation about the project and its potential impacts." (By "misinformation," they usually mean "information.")

As the next chapter will demonstrate, that is exactly what they do.

## Conclusion

In conclusion, the AWEA is what it is: a political lobbying group that will do almost anything to achieve its special-interest goals. It is not an organization characterized by critical thinking, legitimate science, concern for the common good, or genuine concern for nature.

It is characterized by securing dirty profits—profits that never would have occurred on a level playing field of business.

---

[41] Kaplan and Giovanello, *Siting Handbook,* section 7-1 to 7-3.

# — 5 —

# My Story

At this juncture, I could go on as I have to make a compelling case that wind energy is not all that it's cracked up to be. But there is nothing more reliable and easy to understand than an eye-witness account. It seems appropriate to introduce that story here and now.

Few people have had the (dis)pleasure of being offered million-dollar contracts from wind developers, or the experience of watching a rural community dissolve into utter chaos by a single issue. But this is something I can speak to first-hand, and it began with a brief conversation in southeastern South Dakota.

### Enter Big Wind

The first person to approach me was my neighbor.

I think it was in 2010. Although he was not a close friend or relative, he was a good neighbor. He wanted me to sign an easement/lease for wind energy. I wasn't interested for any amount of money for many of the reasons already covered in this book. So, it was naturally a short conversation.

Then, in the summer of 2011, we sold our long-time home in Avon. Although we had some land closer to town that we thought of building on, in 2008 we were fortunate enough to buy 230 acres just a mile from where I grew up. Although there was no water or electricity, it was feasible to install them.

It was a beautiful spot with a 360-degree view. It was also located on a blacktop road with a ¼ mile driveway. My mother and brother lived about a mile away, and I was thankful I could be close to her so my brother and I could take care of her. It really was a perfect spot to retire.

In the spring of 2012, before we broke ground, I called the same neighbor that had tried to buy my easements/lease earlier. I told him I was going to build a new home but would not build it if any wind turbines were coming. He told me to go ahead and build it because all was quiet with the wind industry.

We moved into our new home in September of 2012. After 20 years and many extensions, the federal Production Tax Credit for wind energy expired at the end of 2012, but then, miraculously, it was once again resurrected in an eleventh-hour addendum to the fiscal cliff deal.

On January 1, 2013, the final vote of the 112th Congress secured the extension of the PTC. $12.1 billion dollars for the PTC was included in the bill when it passed at 2am on New Year's Day, 2013. Alongside this most recent extension, a change to the PTC was introduced that relaxed the eligibility requirements for the credit. Renewable energy projects now need only "commence construction" by January 1, 2014, to qualify for the credit, instead of the projects being "placed-in-service" by that date.

Because of the resurrection of the PTC, the Wind Energy Project known as B&H Wind was going to move forward. And the developer's plan that I learned about from that one-day seminar was about to unfold before my eyes.

### The First Project

The developers started with a small group of local investors in 2009 called B&H Wind. With an influx of cash or credit (from an unknown party), they started building the B&H Wind Farm southwest of Tripp and north of Avon in December of 2013. It consisted of forty-three wind turbines at 1.85 MW each. It was to be 79.55 MW to be considered a PURPA "Qualifying Facility" under 80MW.

In August of 2014, before the project was even built, it was sold to Bay Wa. r.e. Wind, a subsidiary of a German company called Bay Wa. It was not built because someone needed more electricity. In fact, Northwestern Energy was forced to buy the electricity under the PURPA law. It was not built because the farmers or the school board were asking for more money. It was built because the production tax credit was extended and investors and developers could use that money to develop this project and make money for themselves.

The project went on line in May of 2015. Around a month or two after the transfer to the German corporation, I happened to drive by my neighbor's place and saw him in the yard. I stopped in. (This foreign ownership really bothered me.) When my neighbor had tried to buy my easements months ago, nothing was ever mentioned that it might end up in foreign hands. All they were pushing at that time was "this is a local project with your friends and neighbors."

I asked him why he didn't mention this when he talked to farmers, many of whom signed up. He was uncomfortable with the conversation (and rightly so). I left.

In July of 2015 it was announced that BayWa r.e. Wind sold the Beethoven project for $143 million to Northwestern Energy. This is the same Northwestern Energy that was forced to buy the electricity generated under the PURPA law. In May of 2015 Northwestern had asked for a rate hike of $26.5 million dollars, or about 20%.

The *Yankton Daily Press and Dakotan* covered the story:

NorthWestern issued a news release Friday announcing the proposed settlement and its acquisition for $143 million of an 80-megawatt wind farm known as Beethoven located near Tripp that was developed by BayWa r.e. Wind. NorthWestern originally sought an annual total rate increase of $26.5 million. The proposed settlement calls for $20.2 million annually, according to the company. The proposed settlement also would allow NorthWestern to collect an additional $9 million annually for the wind-farm purchase. The $9 million would be adjusted after a three-year period to reflect actual costs.[42]

The actual settlement was explained to me by the South Dakota PUC:

The rate increase granted to NorthWestern Energy on October 29, 2015

---

[42] Bob Mercer, "Deal Nearly Complete On Northwestern Rate Request." *Yankton Daily Press and Dakotan* (September 25, 2015).

was approximately $20.9 million. This revenue deficiency includes the costs associated with the Beethoven Wind Farm (a levelized cost of approximately $9.0 million for the first three years) as well as recognition of the elimination of existing Beethoven contracts costs that NorthWestern was paying prior to purchasing the Beethoven Wind Farm. To be clear, the $9.0 million levelized cost for Beethoven is part of the $20.9 million.[43]

To summarize, the B&H Wind, our so-called "friends and neighbors" sold-out to the Germans, who forced Northwestern Energy to buy the electricity. Then, shortly after it started operation, the German company was going to sell it to a multinational corporation, but in the contracts, Northwestern had the first option to buy it—which they did. This allowed them to raise rates; $20 million dollars a year were added to the consumer's electricity bill.

All the while, landowners were under the illusion that "this is local" and "this will save the consumers money."

As heartsick as my wife and I were about this 43-tower wind farm ten miles north of our new home, we thought we could live with it. As I write this, when I sit in my chair at night (which faces north,) I can see the dozens of red blinking lights *ten miles away*. I could not imagine why someone would want to live in the middle of that carnival. I guess it was for the money.

### And Then the Call

In March of 2015, I was out doing an appraisal in Lyman County south of Vivian. I will never forget where I received the phone call just turning back east on I-90 heading for home.

It was a farmer from south of Avon and he was the lead proponent of the wind energy scam ever since it started. We'll call him LP (for Lead Proponent). He asked me if I would be around sometime so he and the Project Manager (we'll call him PM) could come and visit with me. I asked

---

[43] South Dakota PUC. "In the Matter of the Application of Northwestern Corporation DBA Northwestern Energy For Authority to Increase Its Electric Rates." http://www.puc.sd.gov/commission/dockets/electric/2014/EL14-106/memo/memo.pdf

him "visit about what"? I said 'you're not going to build more wind towers, are you?" He said yes. I asked where? He said he didn't know. I said well, if you don't know, why are you calling me? Then, he said it:

*"...we are going to build them all around where you live."*

We've all experienced those punches in the gut in our lives, but this had to be one of the top ten of my life.

I was devastated. This was our dream home a mile from where I grew up. I was a few years from retirement to enjoy my final years here on the plains, and I'm told over the phone that there's a plan to build another *one-hundred*—one-hundred!—massive 1.7-2.5MW turbines north of Avon. That would make a total of 143 towers in the area.

I realize all of this may sound a bit quaint and selfish, protecting *our* privacy, *our* view, *our* home, and so on. But it's not just that. My neighbors love their homes and environment as much as we love ours. There were five new homes built within a few miles of us during the same time period. For a rural area amongst the cornfields and pastures, five new homes is significant. The towers were to go within a mile of Avon, which is a town of about 600 with a lot of retired people that love their homes as much as my neighbors and I love ours.

To reiterate the point of this book: this is a beautiful state and a beautiful area. *How could the promise of money be more important than the quality of life itself?*

Fortunately, I wasn't alone. As months went on and the project turned into a bigger issue than anybody ever suspected, the list of opponents got bigger and bigger...

### The Dreaded Visit

It took me about two weeks to schedule the developers for a local visit. We dreaded the whole thing. They visited us at our home for about four hours. The new project was named "Prevailing Winds." It was planned to have a 200MW capacity and about one-hundred turbines.

We were then shown a map. With sinister clarity that only a real estate appraiser can appreciate, our property and the adjoining land in every direction was visible to everyone. The dots on the map representing wind turbines surrounded our house in every direction.

We then heard about all the economic development, jobs and money for the school and the county and all the other ploys that I could handle. I was even told that I could take the money that I would receive from the proposed lease and go on a mission trip (Marsha and I are active Christians). *Wonderful,* I thought, *drag God into all of this…*

I also had to regularly interrupt the PM for using the phrase "government money" since it's really "*taxpayer* money." After looking at the dots on the map, it was clear that towers were going to be all around us. But, of course, no one would ever come up and just say that. We have windows in every direction of our house because view is very important to us. So he told us the tower that would be to the west (on the neighbor's land) could be tweaked a little bit "*if* we would work with them." I took this as a clear threat.

The best ploy of the day dealt with the dot on the neighbor's land to the northeast. It was on a hill. To block the view of the turbine, he suggested *planting a tree* somewhere between it and our house. Planting a tree! What kind of "tree" in South Dakota is this—which stands taller than the Statue of Liberty?

And then there was the moment when he could see the utter dismay on my wife's (Marsha's) face, and he said, "there's a chance this project won't be built." After they left, she thought maybe this was a note of sympathy. I thought otherwise, and suggested that this, too, was all part of the pitch in manipulating landowners to sign contracts.

Four hours was more than enough. Before they left I asked for a copy of the map.

They refused.

### Economic Reflections on the Offer

It was clear to them that we would not be signing a contract, though we said we'd think about it. The contract was for $2.886 million dollars based on twelve towers over a 25-year period. This estimate included my brother's land.[44]

---

[44] My brother and I are very small operators in today's world of agriculture. Together we

It was clear to me that they were going to offer me what they thought I would take. Their theory is that "everybody has a price." I think that's part of the reason the developers require a confidentiality clause—some landowners get paid more than others because of "their price." They don't want to disclose this price discrimination for the obvious reason that people will feel that they've been treated unfairly.

My brother and I might have had two towers, twelve towers, or no towers. As others did on the first project, they signed up for what they thought was a tower payment and got a small fee for a transmission line. But nothing is guaranteed with these crony-capitalist salesmen. The only thing that is guaranteed is a lower quality of life.

> *"$2.9 million sounds like a lot of money—until dividing it by a quarter-century and surrendering a fourth to Uncle Sam."*

It wasn't even a good deal anyway. $2.9 million sounds like a lot of money—until dividing it by a quarter-century and surrendering a fourth to Uncle Sam. In exceptional seasons, a farmer in South Dakota was making $700 or more net per acre. In 2016, many farmers did well to break even. So, if even a small farmer at 1,000 acres sees their income fluctuate from $0 to $700,000, what is a lease/easement payment of $5-$10,000 a year going to do? (And that's before Caesar takes out his 20-30%.) It's just not that much. It's a wagon load of soybeans.

Somehow, developers make their offers look like a windfall for farmers. I disagree—and there are plenty of other reasons why.

Consider, the farmer has to farm *around* each and every tower. This is annoying enough (especially for those perfectionist farmers who like ultra-straight rows). But if the field has drain tile, it could easily get destroyed during the construction of the turbine. Furthermore, aerial dusters will (and do) refuse to spray crops on lands with turbines. Wind farms are a low-flying pilot's worse nightmare.[45] And then there are

---

own about 1,800 acres, and there's a somewhat elevated a strip that is ½ mile wide and 2 ¾ miles long where we both live.

[45] My son's best friend (and three other South Dakotans) were killed near Highmore, South Dakota, after crashing a small plane into a wind turbine on a cloudy night. See Jonathan Ellis and Terry Vandrovec, "Three cattlemen, former SDSU football player die in plane crash." *Argus Leader* (April 28, 2014). This is by no means the only report of such conflicts between wind turbines and aerial flights.

countless other questions about wind farms' effect on the actual farmlands (what do the underground seismic vibrations do to earthworms and other organic features of the soil? How many birds and bats will be killed by the blades? How will nearby cattle and wildlife respond? Etc.)— none of which include the more obvious problems of multi-mile shadow-flicker during the evening, obtrusive sound, and an overall feeling of enclosure.

I don't know of any landowners that would rent their land out for a *quarter-century*, or a rancher that would contract his calves out for a quarter-century. But wind energy developers talk landowners into signing precisely this type of dangerously foolish contract for wind-rights, and the offers are sweetened with unrealistic monetary projections and numbers that easily mislead.

## What Now?

After the developers finally left our house, we felt defeated. I remember the event so vividly—and all the questions in our minds. *What if they were right? What if everyone around us had signed up? Would we be foolish to say yes, or foolish to say no?*

As farmers, parents, and a married couple, our conversation went something like this: "Well, the kids are gone; we could try to sell the house or move it, and move out of the area. The money would make the rest of the house payments. We've always liked the Black Hills, we could move out there, maybe in a few years my mother and brother would go along." There was little talk of staying here. Hopelessness was the overall tone. We decided to sleep on it.

After sleeping very little, we got up the next morning and joined in the kitchen in our usual way. When Marsha came in I asked, "So, what do you think?" She said without hesitation, "We're going to fight them."

"Me too."

It would be a long road ahead with no certain victory. But why would we ruin our children's inheritance? We love our children and want the best for them.

Why would we transform chunks of the Midwest into an industrial park? This is precious land that we've taken care of for decades, and we take seriously our responsibility before God and humanity to be good stewards of creation.

And why take the risk of having any kind of permanent structure on so much land? Nothing is forever, and yet it is not even within public imagination that wind farms will be taken down—and that this could be a wildly expensive process.

The whole situation caused me to recall a phrase from the 1970s a few years after we married. We were energetic entrepreneurs and eventually found our backs against the wall. My father-in-law, a lanky west river rancher who was as honest and hard working as the day was long said, "Don't let the bastards get you down." That morning, these words seemed particularly appropriate.

And with that, the war began.

# — 6 —

# Prevailing Deceptions

We were out to save our community. Our goal was not necessarily to convince people of all of our views, but to present the truth about the negative aspects of wind energy—including tactics of pressure and disinformation.

It started with letters to the editor and articles in the local paper.[46] All summer (2015) it was back and forth in the paper. Somewhere in the flurry of spilled ink, a few of us got together and decided that if we couldn't stop the developers, then at least we wanted our county zoning to give us some decent setbacks. We had done a lot of research and read horror stories from people in Ontario, New York and other places of how the infrasound affected their health and sleep and how this forced them out of their homes.

So we decided to ask for a 2-mile setback. Our first presentation to the Zoning Board went well. They seemed to listen. A second meeting, not so much, and by the time we were at the third meeting, it was like they weren't even listening.

Big Wind had gotten to them.

---

[46] I refer to the proponents (developers, advocates local and abroad, pro-wind landowners, etc.) as "Big Wind."

## Encounters with Local Caesar

On my first visit to the County Commissioners meeting I naturally asked for a spot to speak. They generally listened, but I was told by the chairman that "everybody had their opinion...*and then there's reality.*" Wow, that's not arrogant at all! Well he was right—and the reality was that the PM (Project Manager) had already convinced the county commissioners to be on his side. In fact, the commissioners, zoning board, zoning administrator *and* the auditor were all in his pocket. He faithfully followed the rules right out of the AWEA *Siting Handbook*.

So after three trips to Zoning—and maybe that many more to the commissioners—I was pretty sick of the politics of the whole thing. I have lived in Bon Homme County all of my life (outside of some military and college time), but I had never been to a County Commissioners meeting. Shame on me! I had always simply trusted them.

By fall, a publication showed up in the paper that there was going to be a hearing on Article 17, "Wind Tower Setbacks." Article 17 specified setbacks from a residence at 1000 ft. and from a property line 500 ft. At this meeting, according to the *Avon Clarion*, over fifty concerned citizens attended and the majority were against the ordinance. Of the fifty people, twelve spoke against Article 17 and two spoke in favor. Those two included one retired farmer and the PM. Ultimately, the Zoning Board ignored the residents and voted for the ordinance promoted by the developer. Cut and dried.

On October 20, 2015 the County Commission held a public hearing on Article 17. Now, over a hundred people were in attendance. Out of the twenty-five people that spoke for the ordinance, at least eighteen (or 72%) of them had a financial vested interest. This meeting was particularly disappointing as I saw the commissioners, some of whom I knew most of my adult life, ignore the residents of the county and side with the developers.

And then to top it all off, the written (form) letters that were sent to the commissioners for their consideration before the meeting were miscounted by the County Auditor in favor of the developer. She counted letters that weren't even opened for the developer. This gave things a slanted appearance.

I documented this fraud and had the South Dakota Department of Criminal Investigation do an investigation of the facts. The Deputy Attorney General's response was:

> The evidence you present simply does not establish the element of criminal intent beyond a reasonable doubt. As such, criminal charges will be declined.
> Thank you for consulting the Attorney General's office in this matter. We encourage people to come forth with evidence of corruption. However, there is nothing further we can do.[47]

That was the end of that. In any case, nine out of ten (90%) of the dissenters were residents near planned turbines. Immediately after everyone spoke, one of the commissioners gave us the tally: 25 for the ordinance, 10 against. In other words, Investors 25, Residents 10.

The Commission passed the ordinance unanimously. The people who spoke for the short setbacks were the investors, the investor's wives, their kids, their parents, the developers, the concrete businesses—all of the people with a financial vested interest. And it was passed to "protect the health, safety and welfare of the County's citizens." This obviously wasn't the case.

Crony-capitalism had simply struck again.

## A Visual Case Study

Below is a photo from one of the Prevailing Winds brochures.

What you'll find in the featured image is not the 500 ft industrial turbines surrounding farms that the company proposes to build. Instead, there' is a picture of a single, 30ft water windmill standing quaintly on the countryside. If this isn't an intentionally misleading strategy, then I don't know what is.

---

[47] Robert Mayer, Office of Attorney General (South Dakota), correspondence to Gregg Hübner (July 6, 2016).

# Prevailing Winds, LLC

A Local Owned and Community Developed
Wind Energy Project

The text below it is from an earlier brochure and it describes our area as "sparsely populated." In the so called "footprint" of the project, which came out months later, we found there were *over two-hundred* homes within the "footprint." For a rural setting, two-hundred homes is anything but "sparsely populated."

And then there's the title: "local owned." How absurd. It is almost certain that the project will be owned by out-of-state or out-of-country corporations within months before or after completing the project. It would have been more accurate to paste a logo of the German or Chinese flag than to mention the words "local owned."[48]

Project Overview
Prevailing Winds is a community developed wind energy project located near Avon, South Dakota in Bon Homme and Charles Mix Counties, with the potential to construct up to 200 megawatts of PTC qualified wind energy by the end of 2016. The project footprint is located on a Coteau which rises 300 to 350 feet above the Choteau Creek Valley along its western boundary and then slowly descends for several miles to the east. The project area is comprised of 45 square miles of sparsely populated agricultural land, centered on the project's point of interconnection. The Coteau's exceptional wind resource, available transmission capacity and welcoming residence make it an ideal location for a wind energy project.

The mission statement of the Prevailing Winds corporation is the following:

> Our commitment is to develop wind energy projects that are sustainable, long term and environmentally sound. We are committed to the social and economic improvement of rural South Dakota by maximizing a projects economic benefit within the local communities.[49]

This all sounds good—and what better way to sell the project than to say it's being built for the "social and economic improvement of rural South Dakota." But as we already know, the wind farm is not being built to harvest electricity or profit landowners—but to harvest the production tax credit and make a profit themselves.

From October 2015 until the Christmas Holidays, it was one letter to the editor after another. Both sides were involved. I now have entire boxes of letters to the editor. At the same time, the developers bought ads in the *Avon Clarion* every week to promote their scam. During the winter of 2015-2016 it got a little quieter. They kept some ads in the paper, but it seemed like life was back to normal just a little. For Marsha, I, and the

---

[48] This appears to be a grammatical error; the Prevailing Winds brochure should have said "locally-owned," not "local owned."
[49] Prevailing Winds LLC, slideshow presentation.
https://puc.sd.gov/commission/dockets/electric/2016/el16-022/presentation.pdf

others, the punch in the gut feeling wasn't there every day like it used to be.

That all changed in July of 2016. The paper came out that the PUC had scheduled their public hearing in Avon on August 24, 2016. Prevailing Winds had submitted their application for the project in June. This was bad news. So the PD put their application into the Public Utilities Commission just in time for them to make their decision before the end of 2016. (Remember, everything the developers do is timed and sized to collect taxpayer money.)

But because this new project was 200 MW, they were required to go through the PUC permitting process. Then they could officially start the project in 2016 and again qualify for the full 100% PTC. On the night of August 24, 2016, the PUC came to Avon, and Big Wind came in like a hurricane.

## The PUC Meeting of 2016

The *Yankton Daily Press and Dakotan* reported three-hundred people; the *Avon Clarion* reported closer to five-hundred. Prevailing Winds gave their presentation and then both proponents and opponents spoke. Although our group of opponents was not that well organized, when it came time to express their opposition, there were a lot more people following this issue than I thought.[50]

It was the same story as the first two meetings. The people that spoke against the project were the people that would have to live with it, and the people that spoke for it were those with fingers in the money pie. We gave it our best effort. But we realized, again, that the deck was stacked against us—this time, on a much larger level than local government.

As far as South Dakota is concerned, Big Wind generally has the county government, along with all three of our federal representatives, in their pocket. As a result, the crony-capitalist wind-developers seem to

---

[50] The full story of the Prevailing Winds project, from initial application to withdrawal of the application on August 30, 2016, can be found at:
https://puc.sd.gov/Dockets/Electric/2016/el16-022.aspx. You can read written comments as well as listen to the actual meeting. I cannot guarantee this will be available any time in the future, but for now it is available and interesting.

have an endless supply of cash—along with lawyers, lobbyists, and a propaganda machine that seems to rarely get questioned. Against such odds, it's easy to get discouraged. But we had to remind ourselves that we had many things working in our favor—not only the prayers of many, but the fact that we're not living under the disorienting cloud of floating dollar signs and crafty salesmen.

Here are some of my remarks from the meeting:

> ...Their main selling points are Economic development, lower electricity rates and money to the school. I am amazed at what the Beethoven Wind Farm has accomplished 10 miles north of here in just one year. The turbines weren't even turning yet last summer when Northwestern Energy applied for a $26.5 million dollar rate hike and the PUC gave them 15.5%. They will spin this to their advantage, but the fact remains Northwestern had not had a rate increase for 35 years and as soon as they were forced to buy the electricity from Beethoven, they asked for a rate hike.
>
> "Economic development," *please*, show me some. Show me a new business in Tripp or Delmont. Show me more jobs. Show me more kids in school. There are none. And lastly money for the school. The Mitchell Daily Republic's headline two-weeks ago was "Tripp Delmont School to consolidate or dissolve." They are broke. I imagined the Tripp Community was promised the same pie in the sky that they are promising us. But that is all that it is: a pie in the sky.

Some of my other comments include the following remarks about "NIMBY":

> One last subject I have is what you have named NIMBY. An acronym for "Not In My Back Yard." Early last year there was a newspaper article where the PUC was quoted as "not considering NIMBY." Not in my back yard doesn't count. I submit to you it does.

> In the last year, I have had two people call me with intentions of building a new home in the area, but would cancel those plans if the project went forward. I have had three families tell me they are moving out of the area if the project is built. I would have never built my house had I known an industrial wind project was coming.

If the county loses real estate taxes on houses left vacant or not built because of NIMBY, they will lose millions of dollars over the next twenty-five years, which is the time frame for all of these so called benefits. Although Prevailing Winds in their brochure calls our area "sparsely populated", there are over 80 homes in the footprint of the project. But it will soon become sparsely populated. Schools are funded on a per student basis. Less students, less money. You can have all the wind turbines you want, if the people leave, you have no students. Case in point, Tripp-Delmont School District. People don't want these in their back yard because they have to hear them, look at them, see their property devalued, they may be forced to leave because of wind turbine syndrome, constant low frequency sound waves that disturb sleep. NIMBY people have issues, and although you say you won't address NIMBY, it's because of these issues people don't want this project. NIMBY IS NOT AN OPINION, NIMBY HAS REAL CONSEQUENCES. Those consequences are: People leave, homes aren't built, tax bases, students in school and local spending all decreases. There is no proof of economic development just promises. What you will get is economic decline. According to your requirements for Prevailing Winds to be permitted, these issues I just mentioned will pose a threat to the social and economic condition of inhabitants or expected inhabitants. These issues will interfere with orderly development of the region. And where is my proof? 10 miles north of here.

All I ask of you tonight is to consider who is for this project and who is against. Decide if you are going to recognize this for what it is, a taxpayer scam, or be part of the scam. The residents who have to live and work in this area that is going to be converted from agricultural/recreational to industrial have not been heard, we have not been protected and we ask you to consider the people, not the promise of money.

After that meeting, I went home feeling we had done about all we could do, and it did seem like the PUC was listening, especially to our plea for proper setbacks.

On August 30, 2016, Prevailing Winds miraculously withdrew its application from the PUC.

Or was it merely the calm before another storm?

In an interview a few days later, the PM was quoted as saying, "the motion to withdraw the application cited misinformation surrounding the project. The organizers said they plan to better inform the community on the wind project and allow Prevailing Winds to revisit their options regarding the project."[51]

But since that day, nearly a year ago, we have not read a single word in the paper or witnessed one scheduled meeting about reaching out to the community to better explain things. Instead, the developers held more sign-up meetings at one of my neighbor's house.

This told me that the reason they pulled their application wasn't because of their poor PR, it was because they didn't have enough farmers signed up to make it work. They just *pretended* they did. (They know the power of peer-pressure.) The PM also said "We don't want to split the community. That's not good for the community," and "the investors didn't intend to reduce the size of the Prevailing Winds projects or break it into smaller parts in order to fall below the threshold requiring PUC approval."

Another lie. On December 27, 2016, the PUC was notified of *thirteen* new projects in Bon Homme and Charles Mix Counties. Each of these projects are under different names, with LP (Lead Proponent) signing every one.

As we already learned, the Beethoven project was built below the capacity threshold so that a utility company like Northwestern could be forced to buy the electricity. The end result of that was not only was the company forced to buy the electricity, they bought the whole wind project and increased their rates so the consumers have to pay for it. Because of the legal disintegration of Prevailing Winds into these thirteen projects, PURPA kicks in so they can do the same thing thirteen times again—resulting in increased rates for thousands of consumers.

In the end, the developers *didn't* do what they said they would (better inform the community), and *did* do what they said they wouldn't (split the community and break up the 200 MW projects into smaller ones).

All of this dishonesty is an integral part of selling wind energy—not a few compromises here and there…

---

[51] Cited in Randy Dockendorf, "New Effort for Wind Facilities Filed with PUC." *Yankton Daily Press and Dakotan* (January 8, 2017).

## The Bluff

I have come to believe that wind developers literally run their whole business model on a bluff. The evidence is straightforward: (1) The AWEA *Siting Handbook*; (2) what I have observed in my own county and home; (3) what people in other counties have told me, as their stories replicate mine.

In May of 2015 there was an article in the *Yankton Daily Press and Dakotan* entitled "Public Utilities Commission Must Give OK to Bon Homme Area Wind Farm."[52] A person reading the article gets the impression that everything is in place and the project is ready to roll. That's precisely the bluff: that everything is ready and it's too late for opposition.

Then I saw the bluff of how developers show people the map with all the wind turbines around their property, and nobody knows if these people are actually signed up or not. In my case, I discovered that one of the dots was on a piece of land where there was no current contract.

Putting this together from the "Playbook" strategies above, we can modify the overall process of the development as follows:

1. Obtain local investors to initiate the process.
2. Send locals to their neighbors to get easements (the locals are trusted more than an outsider).
3. Get the county officials onboard (I've seen this times ten); promise money for the county and the school (who will stand against the school?)
4. Propagate the mantras and induce peer pressure. Host meetings with big giant check blanks filled out with numbers in the millions of dollars that the school will supposedly get over twenty-five or thirty years.
5. Pretend all the while as if all of the landowners are signed up and imply that you're the only person left out.

---

[52] Randy Dockendorf, "Public Utilities Commission Must Give OK To Bon Homme Area Wind Farm," *Yankton Daily Press and Dakotan* (May 22, 2015).

Running through all of this is the belief that farmers have a herd mentality no different than the livestock they maintain. Peer pressure, creating artificial sense of jealousy about who's getting rich, fear of being excluded and missing a big opportunity, and a sense of social obligation to local businesses all combine into a psychological force to be reckoned with. In the end, developers pick off landowners one by one as the project gets closer, just like running cattle into a pen.

> *"In the end, developers pick off landowners one by one as the project gets closer, just like running cattle into a pen."*

Part of this process involves putting articles in the paper, months in advance of any application filed, to make it look like the project is going to happen. On one occasion, the group had an article in the paper telling how a helicopter was going to be flying around to check out the terrain and look for eagle's nests. And sure enough, a few days later, a helicopter was flying over my neighbor's land. This is intimidation.

Then, they established an office in Avon which displayed a "Prevailing Winds" sign.

In the various dialogs the group always bluff about having more land signed up than they actually do. The amount of acres they claim have been secured is always changing. It would be great if the county officials would ask for a list of the leases to confirm the real numbers, but the confidentiality clause in the contracts forbid that.

Finally, they bluff that there is a need for the electricity and that it's already sold.

From the developer side, then, there are two big hurdles that need to be crossed: (1) signing up the landowners and (2) getting the short setbacks they need to make the project economically feasible. It might take a while to sell the electricity or get the investment money rounded up, but if the county laws are in place and the twenty-five year easements are signed, there is plenty of time to handle the rest.

Now as I stated earlier, I believe this is how developers operate by default because that's what I've seen with both the B&H Wind and Prevailing Winds projects. But in the last few months, my list of contacts in other counties has increased considerably. Why?

Because the PTC won't be around forever. There's a big push to build wind projects before the PTC is reduced or phased out altogether. In fact, the estimate for 2017 is supposed to be at 80% of the full 2.3 cents/KWhr. But if I was a betting man, I would bet that most of these 35 projects had enough paperwork done to qualify them for the 100% PTC.

At the time of this writing, I have recently heard from dissenters in Holt and Antelope counties in Nebraska, and Clark, Davison, Walworth and Deuel counties in South Dakota. And of course there is the Lincoln County battle that has been going on for a couple years.[53] Opposition is also growing in Grant, Brown, Brookings, Campbell, Meade and Sanborn counties. I hear the same thing from residents in all of these areas: developers colonize their projects by using the same shady tactics that I've observed.

### "Scam" and "Bribes"?

I want to pause for a moment and qualify the word "scam," because it's a strong term that should not be thrown around lightly.

When I say "wind energy scam" or similar things, I am not saying that the landowner will not actually get any money for the lease, nor am I saying that the investor will not get a return on his or her investment. I am also not saying the school or the county will not get any tax money.

Perhaps it would be accurate to just call it a "taxpayer scam." The projects are built under the guise of producing economic development for the local area, jobs, increasing tax funds for the school and county, and producing lease money to the landowners. These elements of the scam are smoke screens to keep people thinking about immediate, positive features of the deal while the real reason for building them is hidden. It's like a shell game; look over here at this hand while I do the magic with the other hand.

Similarly, I call the promise of money, jobs and economic development "bribe money." Again, "bribe" is a strong term but it is not without good reason. Without the landowners' consent, nothing could be built. Without the County Zoning they need, nothing could be built. But

---

[53] Lincoln County includes part of Sioux Falls, the largest city in the state.

these various parties have to essentially be "paid-off" to make it work. And in the end, the projects aren't built for the county, the school, for jobs, or anything else that's advertised: it's built for the developers and investors themselves. Any benefit for you and I is a *bi-product* of wind energy.

— 7 —

# LESSONS FROM ABROAD

I've never been to Europe and probably never will. But a few years ago, some friends of ours went to Spain and witnessed protests in the streets because of high utility bills.

They were mostly caused by wind energy.

This is a narrative that rarely gets told, but it remains important. Since 1992, when the Production Tax Credit was born, our country has been trying to copy the more socialist countries in Europe. Why, I don't know, because wind energy has been a massive failure overseas.

For this chapter, we only have time to briefly look at four case studies of foreign wind energy: Spain, Germany, Denmark and Australia. In each of these cases, wind energy has failed to fulfill even the most basic of promises—such as cheaper electricity.

## Spain

"New legislation has left one of wind power's biggest and most successful markets in a state of complete paralysis," writes Michael McGovern for *Windpower Monthly*. "Some Spanish developers seriously considering dismantling their projects and selling the turbines on the second-hand market."[54] Key excerpts from this article are found below:

On 9 June the Spanish government rubberstamped its austere and

---

[54] Michael McGovern. "Spain at a Standstill," *Windpower Monthly* (July 31, 2014).

retroactive regulation, slashing income for all existing renewables technologies and ending support mechanisms for new capacity. As a result, the national wind-power market entered a stage of full paralysis, according to practically all speakers at Spanish wind energy association AEE's annual convention, held the following day in Madrid. Since the regulation's draft in January there have been mounting rumors of operators planning to rip out turbines from existing sites in Spain to sell them to more lucrative markets abroad. "There are clients we are talking to about this possibility," confirmed Fernando Ibanez, customer relations manager at Spanish turbine maker Gamesa. Taken from ElPais (Madrid publication in 2014) Spain's electricity bills are among the highest in Europe, having risen 60 percent between 2006 and 2012, with only the Irish and Cypriots paying more. Following two price rises in August and October, electricity companies announced just before Christmas that prices would go up a further 11 percent in January; in the face of the outcry that followed, the government intervened, preventing the increase.[55]

## Germany

To the surprise of many, Germany plans to *stop* building new wind farms by 2019, gradually turning away from its $1.1 trillion wind power program:

The government plans to cap the total amount of wind energy at 40 to 45 percent of national capacity, according to the report. By 2019, this policy would cause a massive reduction of 6,000 megawatts of wind power capacity compared to the end of 2015's capacity. "The domestic market for many [wind turbine] manufacturers collapses completely," Julia Verlinden, a spokesperson for the German Green Party, told Berliner Zeitung. "With their plan, the federal government is killing the wind companies." Verlinden goes on to blame the political influence of "old, fossil fuel power plants." Germany's government, however, has been very supportive of wind power. The government estimates that it will spend over $1.1 trillion financially supporting wind power, even though building wind turbines hasn't achieved the government's goal of actually reducing carbon dioxide ($CO_2$) emissions. Germany created lucrative subsidies and tax benefits for wind power in 2011 after

---

[55] Ibid.

it decided to abandon nuclear power entirely by 2022 following the Fukushima Daiichi nuclear disaster in Japan. German utilities are already suing the government for $21 billion over the nuclear shutdown plan. Electricity from new wind power is nearly four times as expensive as electricity from existing nuclear power plants, according to analysis from the Institute for Energy Research. The rising cost of subsidies is passed onto ordinary rate-payers, which has triggered complaints that poor households are subsidizing the affluent. Nuclear power made up 29.5 percent of Germany's energy in 2000—in 2015, the share dropped down to 17 percent.[56]

## Denmark

In another report from *The Daily Caller,* Michael Bastasch reports on the failure of wind energy in Denmark:

Denmark's government abandoned plans to build five offshore wind power farms Friday amid fears the electricity produced there would become too expensive for Danish consumers.

"Since 2012 when we reached the political agreement, the cost of our renewable policy has increased dramatically," said Climate Minister Lars Christian Lilleholt, a Liberal Party politician representing the country's minority government, according to Reuters. The government would have had to pay $10.63 billion to buy electricity from the five wind farms — a price deemed too expensive for consumers who already face the highest electricity prices in Europe. "We can't accept this, as the private sector and households are paying far too much. Denmark's renewable policy has turned out to be too expensive," Lilleholt said. Denmark gets about 40 percent of its electricity from wind power and has a goal of getting half of its electricity from wind by 2020. But that goal has come up against a stronger prevailing headwind: high energy prices.

Danes have paid billions in taxes and fees to support wind turbines, which has caused electricity prices to skyrocket even as the price of actual electricity has decreased. Now, green taxes make up 66 percent of Danish electricity

---

[56] Andrew Follett, "Germany To Abandon $1.1 Trillion Wind Power Program By 2019," *The Daily Caller* (April 8, 2016).

bills. Only 15 percent of electricity bills went to energy generation. Electricity prices have gotten so high, the government has decided to slash green taxes on consumer energy bills.[57]

Another, more recent article, reveals the same problems:

Denmark's' right-wing government has moved to cancel all offshore wind farms in a bid to lower costly green taxes levied on Danes' electric bills.

"When I think back on the energy agreement from 2012, it was a mistake that we agreed to build the coastal wind turbines," Climate and Energy Minister Lars Christian Lilleholt said Tuesday.

Lilleholt announced he would cancel all coastal wind turbines that were supposed to be built in 2012, and has promised to replace these projects with offshore wind turbines in 2025 as part of the country's plan to lower energy bills — which are among the highest in Europe.[58]

## South Australia

Australia faces the same problems: high electricity and an unreliable power grid:

Wind turbines in South Australia were using more power than they generated during the state's electricity crisis, which has prompted major businesses to threaten shutdowns and smaller firms to consider moving interstate. The sapping of power by the turbines during calm weather on July 7 at the height of the crisis, which has caused a price surge, shows just how unreliable and intermittent wind power is for a state with a renewable energy mix of more than 40 per cent. Australian Industry Group chief executive Innes Willox yesterday said the rise in prices, already the highest in the country, had disrupted industry and served as a warning for the rest of the nation. "That is a serious blow to energy users across SA and has disrupted supply chains upon which thousands of jobs depend," he said. "The real risk is if this volatility becomes the norm across the National

---

[57] Michael Bastasch, "Windswept Denmark Says Wind Energy Has Become Too Expensive," *The Daily Caller* (May 13, 2016).
[58] Michael Bastasch, "Denmark Cancels All Coastal Wind Turbines To Save Taxpayers $1 Billion," *The Daily Caller* (June 7, 2016).

Electricity Market. "In June, electricity cost South Australia $133 per megawatt hour on average — already a high price. But since July 1, electricity prices have spiked above $10,000 per MWh at times."Mr Willox echoed warnings of the South Australian government on the weekend, saying "We will see similar episodes again, and not just in SA", and backing calls for major reform of the NEM.[59]

## Reflections on the Cost of Electricity

The above examples only cover a tiny fraction of the global problems created by wind energy. But the point is clear and undeniable: wind energy is a general failure, as it is almost certain to increase electricity prices and destabilize the power grid.

Tom Stacy, a former member of the ASME Energy Policy Committee, and George Taylor (PhD), the director of Palmetto Energy Research, conducted a study regarding wind energy and the

> *"Wind energy is a general failure, as it is almost certain to increase prices and destabilize the power grid."*

price of electricity.[60] The study "shows that on average, electricity from new wind resources is nearly four times more expensive than from existing nuclear and nearly three times more expensive than from existing coal."[61] This is not a small percentage increase; it's a multi-factor difference.

This is a severe blow to the logic of wind energy. People and government treasuries can only lose so much money for so long.

But this problem gets compounded to the point of absurdity when we realize all the money and wealth destroyed in property devaluation…

---

[59] Michael Owen, "Business blows up as turbines suck more power than they generate," *The Australian* (July 20, 2016).
[60] See Thomas Stacy and George Taylor, "The Levelized Cost of Electricity From Existing Generation Sources." *The Institute for Energy Research* (June 2015).
[61] Institute for Energy Research, Press Release (June 2015). http://instituteforenergyresearch.org/analysis/what-is-the-true-cost-of-electricity/

# — 8 —

# Property Devaluation

I've been doing real estate appraisals since the early 80's and became a Certified General Appraiser in 1992. I have literally done thousands of appraisals in about a twenty-two county area in southeastern, south central and central South Dakota. For many years I did residential, commercial, and agricultural appraisals. In the farm crisis of the 80's I was under contract with the FmHA to do real and chattel appraisals for the government. I could go on, but you get the point: property valuation—especially in the rural Midwest—is "my thing."

The farm crisis of the 1980s wasn't much fun. Bankruptcy, divorce, foreclosures, write offs, mediation, you name it. I've heard all the stories (and there are a *lot* of sad stories out there.) And I have watched other painful stories in a couple documentaries on the wind farm scam, such as *Down Wind* and *Windfall.* These two are probably the best and show the suffering that rural people have experienced when Big Wind built projects too close to them.

In Ontario, the government outright *mandated* certain wind projects, so the landowner was forced to abide and live with it. If it affected their health to the point where they couldn't stand it, their only option was to move out. These health-related issues will be addressed in the next chapter.

For now, I want to address this subject of property devaluation around four key points, the first of which is "the Principle of Substitution."

## 1: The Principle of Substitution

In the field of real estate, there is a law called "The Principle of Substitution." It means that a typical buyer will not pay the same price for a similar house in an area he or she doesn't like if they can buy the same house in an area that they *do* like. Or additionally, a buyer will not pay more for a House A when he can buy House B in the same area for a lesser price.

Relating this to wind energy, would one build or buy a home in an industrial wind park if he could build or buy a similar home where there was no wind park? Of course not. This is a terribly easy concept to grasp, and it directly and immediately alters the value of both land and homes.

## 2: Location, Location, Location

Have you ever heard of this one before? This phrase "location, location, location" reaffirms the Principle of Substitution.

When buying or selling a home, most of the time, the most important deciding factor is *location*. Since our experience fighting Big Wind, I have had two calls from people thinking about building new homes. But (surprise!) they were not going to build if a wind project was coming. Marsha and I certainly wouldn't have built a new home had we known someday it would be surrounded by dozens of rotating skyscrapers.

We have since had a number of families tell us that they will simply move out if the wind project of 100 towers is built. People generally hate moving, so this was apparently a decisive factor for them.

## 3: Professional Studies on Property Devaluation

I'm not alone in suggesting that wind farms decrease the value of homes and land.

Appraisal Group One conducted a study in 2009 in the state of Wisconsin. Their conclusions were that:

A. In *all* cases with a 1-5 acre residential property, whether vacant or improved, there will be a negative impact in property value.

B. With 1-5 acre properties the negative impact in property value in bordering proximity ranged from -39% to -43%.

C. With 1-5 acre properties the negative impact in property value in close proximity ranged from -33% to -36%.

D. With 1-5 acre properties the negative impact in property value in near proximity ranged from -24% to -29%.

E. In all cases the estimated loss of value between the vacant land and improved property was close, however the vacant land estimates were always higher by a few percentage points.

F. It appears that hobby farm use on larger parcels would have lesser sensitivity to the proximity of wind turbines than single family land use

G. Placement either in front or at the rear of a residence has similar negative.[62]

In 2010, Jennifer Hinman submitted a master's thesis for her Applied Economics graduate degree entitled "Wind Farm Proximity and Property Values." Her results?

> The estimation results provide evidence that a location effect exists such that before the wind farm was even approved, properties located near the eventual wind farm area were devalued in comparison to other areas. Additionally, the results show that property value impacts vary based on the different stages of wind farm development.[63]

In 2014, Stephen Gibbons of the London School of Economics published a landmark study entitled "Gone With the Wind: Valuing the Visual Impacts of Wind Turbines through House Prices." The abstract is:

> This study provides quantitative evidence on the local benefits and costs of wind farm developments in England and Wales, focussing on their

---

[62] Kurt C. Kielisch, "Wind Turbine Impact Study," *Appraisal Group One* (September 9, 2009).

[63] Jennifer Hinman, "Wind Farm Proximity and Property Values: A Pooled Hedonic Regression Analysis of Property Values in Central Illinois." (MS Thesis for Illinois State University, May 2010).

visual environmental impacts. In the tradition of studies in environmental, public and urban economics, housing costs are used to reveal local preferences for views of wind farm developments. Estimation is based on quasi-experimental research designs that compare price changes occurring in places where wind farms become visible, with price changes in appropriate comparator groups. These comparator groups include places close to wind farms that became visible in the past, or where they will become operational in the future and places close to wind farms sites but where the turbines are hidden by the terrain. All these comparisons suggest that wind farm visibility reduces local house prices, and the implied visual environmental costs are substantial.[64]

How substantial? *The Daily Mail* reports on the study:

The study by the London School of Economics (LSE) – which looked at more than a million sales of properties close to wind farm sites over a 12-year period – found that values of homes within 1.2 miles of large wind farms were being slashed by about 11 per cent.
This means that if such a wind farm were near an average house in Britain, which now costs almost £250,000, it would lose more than £27,000 in value.

In sought-after rural idylls where property prices are higher, the financial damage is even more substantial. In villages around one of Southern England's largest onshore developments – Little Cheyne Court Wind Farm in Romney Marsh, Kent, where homes can cost close to £1 million – house values could drop by more than £100,000. The study further discovered that even a small wind farm that blighted views would hit house values.

Homes within half a mile of such visible turbines could be reduced in value by about seven per cent. Even those in a two-and-a-half-mile

---

[64] Stephen Gibbons, "Gone with the Wind: Valuing the Visual Impacts of Wind Turbines Through House Prices." *Spatial Economic Research Center Discussion Paper 159* (April 2014).

radius experienced price reductions of around three per cent.[65]

In 2012, Lansink Appraisals and Consulting conducted a study in Canada entitled "Diminution in Price: Melancthon and Clear Creek Wind Turbine Analysis."[66] Of the properties they studied, the average decline in value was a whopping 35-38%.

In 2011, Martin Heintzelman of the Clarkson University School of Business and Carrie Tuttle of Clarkson University, published an article in *Land Economics* called "Values in the Wind." Their conclusion?

> The siting of wind facilities is extremely controversial. This paper uses data on 11,369 property transactions over 9 years in Northern New York to explore the effects of new wind facilities on property values. We use a repeat-sales framework to control for omitted variables and endogeneity biases. We find that nearby wind facilities significantly reduce property values. Decreasing the distance to the nearest turbine to 1 mile results in a decline in price of between 7.73% and 14.87%. These results indicate that there remains a need to compensate local homeowners/communities for allowing wind development within their borders.[67]

In 2010, the appraiser Michael McCann testified to the Adams County Board about property devaluation due to wind farms. His conclusions?

> 1. Residential property values are adversely and measurably impacted by close proximity of industrial-scale wind energy turbine projects to the residential properties, with value losses measured up to 2-miles from the nearest turbine(s), in some instances.
> 2. Impacts are most pronounced within "footprint" of such projects, and many ground-zero homes have been completely unmarketable, thus depriving many homeowners of reasonable market-based liquidity or pre-existing home equity.

---

[65] Sanchez Manning, "Proof wind turbines take thousands off your home: Value of houses within 1.2 miles of large wind farms slashed by 11%, study finds." *The Daily Mail* (January 27, 2014).
[66] Ben Lansink, "Diminution in Price: Melancthon and Clear Creek Wind Turbine Analysis." Lansink Appraisals and Consulting (October, 2012).
[67] Martin D Heintzelman and Carrie Tuttle, "Values in the Wind: A Hedonic Analysis of Wind Power Facilities" *Land Economics* (July 15, 2011).

3. Noise and sleep disturbance issues are mostly affecting people within 2-miles of the nearest turbines and 1-mile distances are commonplace, with many variables and fluctuating range of results occurring on a household by household basis.

4. Real estate sale data typically reveals a range of 25% to approximately 40% of value loss, with some instances of total loss as measured by abandonment and demolition of homes, some bought out by wind energy developers and others exhibiting nearly complete loss of marketability.

5. Serious impact to the "use & enjoyment" of many homes is an on-going

occurrence, and many people are on record as confirming they have rented other dwellings, either individual families or as a homeowner group-funded mitigation response for use on nights when noise levels are increased well above ambient background noise and render their existing homes untenable.

6. Reports often cited by industry in support of claims that there is no property value, noise or health impacts are often mischaracterized, misquoted and/or are unreliable. The two most recent reports touted by wind developers and completed in December 2009 contain executive summaries that are so thoroughly cross-contingent that they are better described as "disclaimers" of the studies rather than solid, scientifically supported conclusions. Both reports ignore or fail to study very relevant and observable issues and trends.

7. If Adams County approves a setback of 1,000 feet, 1,500 feet, or any distance less than 2-miles, these types of property use and property value impacts are likely to occur to the detriment of Adams County residences and citizens for which the nearest turbines are proposed to be located.

8. The approval of wind energy projects within close proximity to occupied homes is tantamount to an inverse condemnation, or regulatory taking of private property rights, as the noise and impacts are in some respects a physical invasion, an easement in gross over neighboring properties, and the direct impacts reduce property values and the rights of nearby neighbors.

9. A market value reduction of $6.5 million is projected for the residential property located in the footprint and within 2-miles of the

pending Prairie Mills project located in east Adams County.[68]

The evidence is clear: *wind farms substantially devalue property.*

Are there dissenting studies? Not many, but there are some. As any research or scientist knows, numbers can be manipulated—especially when there's money behind it.

> *"The evidence is clear: wind farms substantially devalue property."*

One dissenting study took place in 2009 published by the Ernest Orlando Lawrence Berkeley National Laboratory. It suggests that the decrease in land values are statistically insignificant. Aside from the limitations of this study, one should note the crony-capitalism evident on the front page (which reads in the footer):

> The work described in this report was funded by the Office of Energy Efficiency and Renewable Energy (Wind & Hydropower Technologies Program) of the U.S. Department of Energy under Contract No. DE-AC02-05CH1123.[69]

Directly funded by a federal wind program? This doesn't seem very "neutral" and "unbiased" to me. In any case, this research certainly is a deviation from all the other studies done—not to mention a deviation from common sense.

All I have personally heard Big Wind say about property devaluation is that they have one study in Colorado where prices weren't affected by industrial wind energy systems. If you keep up with the Colorado real estate market, prices have been increasing 12% a year or better, but most of this increase is because of marijuana laws and other variables.

---

[68] Michael McCann, "Testimony of Michael McCann on property value impacts in Adams County IL." *Wind Action* (June 8, 2010).
[69] Ben Hoen, Ryan Wiser, et. al., "The Impact of Wind Power Projects on Residential Property Values in the United States: A Multi-Site Hedonic Analysis." *Ernest Orlando Lawrence Berkeley National Laboratory* (December 2009).

## 4: Effects of the Lease

A final concern has to do with legal strings attached to wind-rights contracts.

If you have never read a lease/easement from a wind developer, you should. The leases are long, complicated and confusing to the average layman. This is probably intentional. In any case, there are a few key features worth noting.

First, the lease can be transferred to a 2nd party, and many times once it goes to the 2nd tenant, or owner of the wind turbine, it takes the 1st party off the hook for any claims made by the landlord (the landowner). As we already learned, most often, wind projects are owned by foreign or multinational corporations. Landowners are going to have a hard time getting anywhere if there is an issue that needs to be resolved.

Second, there is the notorious "confidentiality clause." This must be read *very* carefully. Usually it forbids landowners from telling anybody how much they are getting paid for the lease. I have even read about leases in Nebraska that would not let a prospective buyer see the terms of the lease until after closing!

*Figure 8.1: Sample Contract*

13.2   **Confidentiality**. Landowner shall maintain in the strictest confidence, for the benefit of Lessee, any Assignee or Tenant, all information pertaining to the financial terms of or payments under this Agreement, Lessee's site or product design, methods of operation, methods of construction, power production or availability of the Windpower Facilities, and the like, whether disclosed by Lessee, any Assignee or Tenant, or discovered by Landowner, unless such information either (i) is in the public domain by reason of prior publication through no act or omission of Landowner or its employees or agents; or (ii) was already known to Landowner at the time of disclosure and which Landowner is free to use or disclose without breach of any obligation to any person or entity. Landowner shall not use such information for its own benefit, publish or otherwise disclose it to others, or permit its use by others for their benefit or to the detriment of Lessee, any Assignee or Tenant. Notwithstanding the foregoing, Landowner may disclose such information to Landowner's lenders, attorneys, accountants and other personal financial advisors solely for use in connection with their representation of Landowner regarding this Agreement; any prospective purchaser of the Property who has made a written offer to purchase or otherwise acquire the Property that Landowner desires to accept; or pursuant to lawful process, subpoena or court order requiring such disclosure, provided Landowner in making such disclosure advises the party receiving the information of the confidentiality of the information and obtains the written agreement of said party not to disclose the information, which agreement shall run to the benefit of and be enforceable by Lessee. Landowner shall get Lessee's written consent before issuing a press release or having any contact with or responding to the news media with any operational, sensitive or confidential information with respect to this Agreement, the wind power project to be constructed on the Property by Lessee, or any other existing wind power project owned or operated by Lessee. The provisions of this Section 13.2 shall survive the termination or expiration of this Agreement.

This was actually the case in the lease offered to me. It stated that a prospective buyer could not see the terms of the lease until the purchase agreement was signed. (Talk about a legal trap!) My biggest fear was that the terms would prevent me (or my heirs) from selling the property on the open market or by public auction. In any case, no informed buyer would sign a purchase agreement—including a 30 to 40-year contract!—without knowing what was included in in it. The very concept is unthinkable.

The possibility also exists that a landowner might sign an easement/lease and the project isn't built. This lease might still extend out 20 to 40 years, and even though nothing is built now, somebody might decide to put a wind turbine on their land years down the road. This would be similar to the ranchers in North Dakota that were having a quiet, peaceful life on their ranch only to find out they don't own the mineral rights, and one day the well drillers are driving across their land and digging wells.

When I consulted with two local attorneys about these leases, they both told me the same thing: *Don't sign it.*

## Conclusion

To conclude this chapter, just ask yourself this simple question: Would you rather live where you presently live (without wind turbines) or would you rather live within an industrial wind project?

The chances are probably 100% that any potential buyer for your home would agree with you.

# — 9 —

# Effects on the Environment and Human Health

Let's briefly recap what we've covered so far:

A. Wind energy (as it currently exists) is crony-capitalism *par excellence*. It's a corrupt and unjust way of doing business.
B. Wind energy is terribly inefficient and uninvestable.
C. As such, wind energy cannot survive without taxpayer help, which includes things like subsidies and tax credits for crony-capitalists.
D. Wind energy tends to destabilize the power grid and raise electricity prices.
E. Wind energy advocates are chiefly motivated by their own desire for profit, not about the community or landowners.
F. Wind energy decreases the value of large masses of land by a significant percentage.
G. Wind-rights contracts are very, *very* risky.

Now, for item H: *wind energy is bad for the environment and human health*.

This is probably the most debated subject related to wind energy. The reason for this largely stems from the belief that wind-energy is "green," and that this is the entire purpose for its existence.

We've already shown this second idea to be untrue in previous chapters. Wind energy exists to profit crony-capitalists. But, as it has been shown by others before, even the first idea ("green" energy) proves to be untrue as well. Wind energy is bad for the environment and human health.

In this chapter we'll explore this expansive topic in two general areas: negative effects on the environment, and its subset, negative effects on human health.

## Negative Effects on the Environment

Out of all the potential (and actual) negative effects on the environment, the most evident and indisputable is the death of birds and bats.

Thousands and thousands of bats and birds are killed from wind turbines every year. As we learned, the blades of the tower itself spin very fast, which either kills the airborne creature upon impact, or disorients it into a fatal-fall. The result is a regular, systematic source of unnecessary animal death.

This isn't a problem just because it's "not nice." It's a problem because it has negative effects on an ecosystem. Like any animal, birds and bats are an integral part of any ecosystem; one cannot significantly disrupt one part of an ecosystem without effecting other parts (and the whole). This may involve significant practical costs. Without ants, for example, most of the world would be buried in waste. Ants therefore "save trillions" in waste disposal. Similarly, "The U.S. Geological Survey says the value of pest-control services to US agriculture provided by bats ranges from $3.7 billion to as much as $53 billion yearly."[70] Bats in particular control insect (e.g., mosquito) populations, and larger birds feed on rodents and other critters that would otherwise spiral out of balance in a population. If one is concerned about the "environment" on any degree whatsoever, then these types of ecological effects must be taken into account one way or another.

Christopher Hooker wrote about this in a 2010 piece in *The Daily Telegraph:*

> In all my scores of items over the years on why the obsession with wind turbines will be seen as one of the major follies of our age, there is one issue I haven't touched on. The main practical objection to turbines, of

---

[70] Mark Duchamp, "Wind turbines are actually slaughtering millions of birds and bats annually." Save the Eagles International.

course, is that they are useless, producing derisory amounts of electricity at colossal cost. (Yet the Government wants us to spend £100 billion on building thousands more of them which, even were it technically possible, would do virtually nothing to fill the fast-looming 40 per cent gap in our electricity supply.)

A feature of these supposedly environment-friendly machines that I haven't mentioned, however, is their devastating effect on wildlife, notably on large birds of prey, such as eagles and red kites. Particularly disturbing is the extent to which the disaster has been downplayed by professional bodies, such as the Royal Society for the Protection of Birds in Britain and the Audubon Society in the US, which should be at the forefront of exposing this outrage, but which have often been drawn into a conflict of interest by the large sums of money they derive from the wind industry itself.

There is plenty of evidence for the worldwide scale of this tragedy. The world's largest and most carefully monitored wind farm, Altamont Pass in California, is estimated to have killed between 2,000 and 3,000 golden eagles alone in the past 20 years. Since turbines were erected on the isle of Smola, off Norway, home to an important population of white-tailed sea eagles, destruction is so great that last year only one chick survived. Thanks to wind farms in Tasmania, a unique sub-species of wedge-tailed eagles faces extinction. And here in Britain, plans to build eight wind farms on the Hebridean islands, among Scotland's largest concentration of golden eagles, now pose a major threat to the species' survival in the UK.[71]

These negative effects are routinely dismissed as being "insignificant" when compared to other sources of death (e.g., predation). This is untrue and misleading for two reasons: (1) the deaths involve *endangered species* and (2) the *statistics are inaccurate* because of their method of data collection (namely, excluding thousands of bird carcasses from the wind-turbine cause). Research from the last five years has brought these realities to light. One 2016 study conducted in Ontario reveals some disturbing

---

[71] Christopher Booker, "Wind turbines: 'Eco-friendly' - but not to eagles." *The Daily Telegraph* (March 13, 2010).

results[72]:

### Ontario

Table 11: Bat species found at wind power projects in Ontario based on fractional ranking and percent species composition.

| | Rank | Species | Percent Composition |
|---|---|---|---|
| Endangered species | 1 | hoary bat | 28.8% |
| | 2 | eastern red bat | 22.8% |
| | 3 | big brown bat | 17.5% |
| | 4 | silver-haired bat | 18.5% |
| | 5 | little brown myotis | 11.7% |
| | 6 | northern long-eared myotis | 0.24% |
| | 7 | tri-coloured bat | 0.19% |
| | 8 | eastern small-footed bat | 0.04% |

In Ontario, the penalty for any individual who kills a single bird from the endangered species list can face a fine of up to $1 million. Wind developers kill *hundreds* as a matter of course—but (like in the U.S.) they are exempt from all such fines.

Just days before leaving the Oval Office, President Obama caved in to Big Wind by allowing each developer to slaughter 4,200 bald eagles and golden eagles for 30-year wind projects. This was a revision to the 2009/2014 law for 5-year projects. The story was covered in the *Washington Times*:

> Bald and golden eagles may be legally killed or injured in the thousands by high-speed turbines (reaching speeds up to 170 miles per hour), under new regulations released Wednesday by the Obama administration. The rules, which affect individual wind-energy companies that plan to operate the technology for up to 30 years, allows up to 4,200 of the birds to perish...The U.S. population of bald eagles stands at roughly 143,000, while the Fish and Wildlife Service puts the number of golden eagles at 40,000....[73]

[72] Bird Studies Canada, Canadian Wind Energy Association, Environment Canada an Ontario Ministry of Natural Resources, "Wind Energy Bird and Bat Monitoring Database Summary of the Findings from Post-construction Monitoring Reports." (July 2016). https://www.bsc-eoc.org/resources/wind
[73] Douglas Ernst, "Obama admin regulation allows wind turbines to kill up to 4,200 bald eagles per company." *Washington Times* (December 14, 2016).

4,200 endangered bird-deaths per company is bigger than it sounds. There are nearly a dozen such "companies," which means (for ten) a whopping 42,000 bald and golden eagles are permitted to be killed by wind developers. If a non-developer killed just *one* bald eagle, she or he fine can be up to $250,000 and face two years of imprisonment. But if they are slaughtered large-scale by crony-capitalists, guess what? The penalty is nothing.

The 4,200 "limit," of course, is fake. We learned that wind developers sneak out of regulations (e.g., PURPA MW capacity) by breaking up their corporations into smaller ones. They can do the same here. If it is discovered that a wind energy company killed more than the "approved" amount of endangered species, they can simply hire a lawyer to split the company up into another, doubling their limit of kills. The policies put in place is cleverly designed to do just that; it satisfies two parties at once: (a) it makes it look like a restriction to protect the environment (to placate the environmentalists) when (b) it practically allows developers to kill as many endangered birds as they need (to placate—and receive cash from—the crony-capitalists).[74]

> "*The policies put in place...practically allows developers to kill as many endangered birds as they need.*"

This reality is compounded by the fact that the counting of carcasses is skewed. The study above in Ontario only included carcasses found within a 50-meter radius of the tower. But the study itself says "the proportion of carcasses expected to fall outside of 50 m to be up to 51.8% of birds, based on 4 studies that searched a radius up to 85 m."[75] Over half! In other words, all the figures should be *increased by a factor of two*. This results in the following deaths of bird in Ontario due to wind energy (over the seven-year period of the study):

---

[74] "Government decisions favor the side with the most political power." Richard Stroup, *Eco-Nomics: What Everyone Needs to Know About Economics and the Environment* (Washington D.C.: Cato Institute, 2003), 24.
[75] Ibid., 36.

A. 61,984 bat carcasses.
B. 21,470 bird carcasses.
C. 701 raptor carcasses.[76]

This is not an "insignificant" amount of wildlife!

Another 2016 study, this time conducted by Purdue University, revealed that the deaths of birds is also far worse than imagined because they aren't restricted to any particular locality:

> Using DNA from tissue and stable isotopes from the feathers of golden eagle carcasses, researchers from Purdue University and the U.S. Geological Survey found that golden eagles killed at the Altamont Pass Wind Resource Area in northern California can come from hundreds of miles away. Golden eagles are a species of conservation concern, so understanding population-level differences and how individuals interact with turbines is key to meeting a U.S. Fish and Wildlife Service target of no net loss to their populations.

> The APWRA is one of the oldest wind farms in the country and one of the largest in the world originally with around 5,000 turbines. Worldwide, such facilities have been responsible for the deaths of 140,000 to 328,000 birds and 500,000 to 1.6 million bats, raising questions about their effects on population sustainability.[77]

In other words, *wind farms kill birds from all over the region*, not birds that just live around wind farms.

The bird/bat issue is just one of the more well-known negative effects of wind energy. Aside from this, there are the other potential negative effects on the environment mentioned earlier: long-term effects on the quality of soil (extremely important for farmers), on wildlife (including livestock), plant life, and so on—mostly from seismic waves in the ground and noise. These are more mysterious and have not been studied. But they introduce more and more dimensions of risk for a form of energy that is supposedly "green."

---

[76] Ibid., multiplying the numbers in this study by 2.
[77] Purdue University, "Wind turbines killing more than just local birds." *Science Daily* (September 29, 2016).

## Human Health Effects: What "Evidence" Counts?

The most immediate and important environmental effect is on human health. Landowners and nearby residents could sleep soundly and had no consistent headaches/dizziness *before* the towers were built, and now, *after* the towers were built, they cannot sleep and have more headaches/dizziness than ever before. These symptoms are almost certainly due to the noise and vibration produced by the turbines. But it doesn't matter which aspect of the wind farm caused it: the effects are real.

Or are they? Advocates of wind energy regularly dismiss these claims as invalid, being "isolated incidents" and "without empirical or scientific basis." Big Wind has even gone as far to plug studies that try to demonstrate that this experience is "all in their head." Supposedly, landowners *imagine* that they're losing sleep and having headaches because of industrial wind turbines. One researcher brings up this topic in the academic journal *Nature and Society*:

> *"Supposedly, landowners imagine that they're losing sleep and having headaches because of industrial wind turbines."*

Where noise problems are acknowledged, some academics such as Professors Simon Chapman at the University of Sydney and Keith Petrie at the University of Auckland subscribe to the mass hysteria ideas promoted by controversial British psychiatrist Simon Wessely. Such assessments primarily implicate people's fears and anxieties about new technologies to explain noise complaints and sleeping difficulties that appear in conjunction with wind farm developments. [I am not persuaded by such arguments, given the seriousness of some of the adverse health effects observed.][78]

Yes, perhaps residents in Ontario, South Dakota, and other rural areas colonized by wind energy are experiencing "mass hysteria." All of us

---

[78] Murray May, "Wind Power Controversy," *Nature and Society* (November-October, 2011).

farmers and rural folk are delusional and have just lost our minds!

It is amazing that this line of thinking also appears in an article published in the *Journal of Health Psychology*.[79] It's also a point in the infamous 2014 pro-wind study (see end of chapter). The logic of the argument is this:

1. Premise: Dizziness and lack of sleep can be categorized as "annoyance."
2. Premise: "Annoyance" can encompass things like psychosis, mass hysteria, and personality traits/disorders.
3. Conclusion: Therefore, negative complaints about new and/or local wind turbines can be legitimately dismissed and ignored. ("It's just in your head!")

The problem, of course, is that dizziness and lack of sleep cannot simply be lumped together with things like personality and hysteria. But, as unjustified as this line of thinking is, it remains part of the Big Wind rhetoric in one situation to the next.

Another desperate excuse by Big Wind is that "there's simply no evidence for negative health effects on humans." You might be thinking, *what about all the people who are experiencing these effects every day? Isn't that sufficient "evidence?"* According to Big Wind, no. All of this eye-witness, first-hand experience is dismissed as "anectodal." These are isolated incidents, and they also (supposedly) don't make up "hard data."

Here, the demands by Big Wind start to look ridiculous. First, they forget that these are landowners who have more than likely signed legal contracts not to complain. This should amplify the weight of those that *do* complain, because such landowners could be taking a huge personal risk by doing so.

Second, the claim about there not being "hard data" and "academic

---

[79] "Symptom expectations were created by viewing information readily available on the Internet, indicating the potential for symptom expectations to be created outside of the laboratory, in real world settings. Results suggest psychological expectations could explain the link between wind turbine exposure and health complaints." Fiona Crichton, George Dodd, Gia Schmid, Greg Gamble, and Keith Petrie, "Can expectations produce symptoms from infrasound associated with wind turbines?" *Journal of Health Psychology* 33:4 (Apr 2014): 360-364.

studies" is misleading. How many peer-review articles are there that demonstrate the negative health effects of thrusting one's head into a pot of boiling tar? None. This kind of study has *never* been conducted, much less published. No data has been collected. No professional committee has reviewed it. No one has *ever* conducted this kind of experiment—whether in a randomized clinical trial, double-blind study, or otherwise, whether in the UK, Australia, the US, or China, whether in the past decade, or the past century. Therefore, we have to say that "there is no evidence proving that there are negative health effects by thrusting one's head into a pot of boiling tar."

But that's irrelevant! Data doesn't matter at this point. What matters most is first-hand experience and reasonable inferences based on this experience. One can reasonably conclude that putting your head in a pot of boiling tar is going to harm you, regardless if there are any "studies" supporting this conclusion or not—and regardless if anyone has physically tried this or not.

In the same way, to demand "evidence" and "data" that "proves" that wind turbines create negative health effects is often a superficial demand—especially when *there are* "eye-witness accounts" and "first-hand experience" that testify. (See Appendix A for a snapshot of some of these horror stories.) People's own experiences are sufficient, and they won't just go away with the dismissive wave of a hand.

Furthermore, the argument cuts both ways: if Big Wind wants to say there is no evidence showing the harm of wind turbines, where is the evidence showing the *safety* of wind turbines? This point was made in a 2011 literature review in the *Bulletin of Science, Technology, and Society*, which examined low-frequency noise (or "infrasound"):

> In a search of the literature, no studies were found which come close to replicating the long-term exposures to low level infrasound experienced by those living near wind turbines. So, to date, there are no published studies showing that such prolonged exposures do not harm humans.[80]

The burden of proof is on the developer as much as it is the landowners

---

[80] Alec Salt and James Kaltenbach, "Infrasound from Wind Turbines Could Affect Humans," *Bulletin of Science, Technology, and Society*. 31:4 (2011):296-302.

and residents. *Where is the data and literature* that strongly shows that there are no negative health effects on humans from wind turbines? Wind developers are responsible for demonstrating the safety of their business if there are complaints about property-rights infringement.

> Dr. William H. Stewart, the former Surgeon General of the United States, in a keynote talk to a 1969 Conference on Noise as a Public Health Hazard stated the following: "Must we wait until we prove every link in the chain of causation? In protecting health, absolute proof comes late. To wait for it is to invite disaster or to prolong suffering unnecessarily.[81]

This is an important point: if we wait to collect the *perfect data* and create the *perfect study* for evaluating all the effects of wind energy, we'll be waiting forever. In the meantime, the lives of thousands of residents are destroyed. It will be too "late," as the General Surgeon said.

> *"Wind developers are responsible for demonstrating the safety of their business if there are complaints about property-rights infringement."*

The Surgeon General isn't alone. Many scholars suggest that wind energy is premature and that we must conduct more studies. "Assessing the effects of wind turbines on human health," writes two scientists in *Environmental Health*, "is an emerging field and conducting further research into the effects of wind turbines (and environmental changes) on human health, emotional and physical, is warranted."[82] Or consider, three other intellectuals writing in the journal *Noise and Health*: "Further research is needed to determine at what distances risks become negligible, as well as to better estimate the portion of the population suffering from adverse effects at a given distance."[83] Or consider the very specific areas needing research in an article by Max Whisson in *Nature and Society*:

---

[81] Arline Bonzaft, "The Noise from Wind Turbines: Potential Adverse Impacts on Children's Well-Being," *Bulletin of Science, Technology and Society* 31 (July 20, 2011): 391.

[82] Loren Knopper and Christopher Ollson, "Health effects and wind turbines: A review of the literature." *Environmental Health* 10:78 (2011).

[83] Michael Nissenbaum, Jeffrey Armanini, Christopher Hanning, "Effects of industrial wind turbine noise on sleep and health," *Noise and Health* 14:60. (2012): 237-243.

...it seems obvious to me that there is a very urgent need to study disease rates and death rates in the areas near wind farms and in controlled areas more than 10 km away. There is also an urgent need to organise clinical and epidemiological studies to seek further evidence of the diseases and pathology described in the studies of industrial Vibro Acoustic Disease. There is similarly a very urgent need for veterinarians and ecologists to follow up the reports from farmers all around the world of abnormalities in farm animals near current large wind turbines, as with chickens that are hatching with crossed beaks and other abnormalities, and stock of many types being born with unusual abnormalities. Above all I feel that there is an urgent need to study the epidemiology of organisms that live in the soil and water around wind farms. These organisms are known to communicate by low frequency vibration. All of this must be correlated with precise measurements of noise and vibration associated with wind turbine operation. Such measurements must be made on the turbine towers, on surrounding soils and on surrounding buildings out to at least 10 km.[84]

Notice what is *not* said in all three of these publications: "wind energy is definitely safe and we should support it." No one can credibly make this claim. That's why almost no scientist, doctor, or professor does.

Carl Phillips rightly summarizes this whole situation:

There is overwhelming evidence that wind turbines cause serious health problems in nearby residents, usually stress-disorder-type diseases, at a nontrivial rate. The bulk of the evidence takes the form of thousands of adverse event reports. There is also a small amount of systematically gathered data. The adverse event reports provide compelling evidence of the seriousness of the problems and of causation in this case because of their volume, the ease of observing exposure and outcome incidence, and case-crossover data. Proponents of turbines have sought to deny these problems by making a collection of contradictory claims including that the evidence does not "count," the outcomes are not "real" diseases, the outcomes are the victims' own fault, and that acoustical models cannot explain why there are health problems so the problems must not exist. These claims appeared to have swayed many

---

[84] Max Whisson, "Wind Power and Ecology," *Nature and Society* (Nov-Oct, 2011).

nonexpert observers, though they are easily debunked.

Moreover, though the failure of models to explain the observed problems does not deny the problems, it does mean that we do not know what, other than kilometers of distance, could sufficiently mitigate the effects. There has been no policy analysis that justifies imposing these effects on local residents. The attempts to deny the evidence cannot be seen as honest scientific disagreement and represent either gross incompetence or intentional bias.[85]

That's right: as it turns out, the "hard-evidence" *does* point to negative health effects on humans. Let's take a quick look.

## Human Health Effects: The "Hard Evidence"

In June of 2009, a group of scientists presented their results of a study of seismic vibrations at the Third International Meeting on Wind Turbine Noise in Aalborg, Denmark. If people claimed to be feeling or hearing noise from wind farms, this could easily be tested with comparative seismic and acoustic measurements. Here are their conclusions:

> Seismic and acoustic measurements were undertaken at a residential site at the base of the Tararua Ranges close to a windfarm to determine whether nuisance noise reported by the residents could be detected and whether it could be traced to the windfarm.
> Extraneous events were eliminated from the measurements by using only night time records, by removing known events and by eliminating events that did not correlate with the timing of the residents' perception.
> The remaining events were characterised by bursts of around 10 seconds duration and with broad peaks in the power spectra at 28Hz and 10Hz.
> When the residents were played these events, through earbuds or a stereo system, they decided that they were closely similar to the noise

---

[85] Carl Phillips, "Properly Interpreting the Epidemiologic Evidence About the Health Effects of Industrial Wind Turbines on Nearby Residents." *Bulletin of Science, Technology, and Society.* 31:3 (2011):303-315.

they had been reporting. We therefore conclude that the noise 'perceived' by the residents is measurable, consists of separate acoustic and seismic parts and can cause annoyance by disturbing sleep.[86]

This fits with the remarks of a 2014 publication in *Environmental Health Perspectives:*

Large-scale wind turbines are a relatively recent innovation, so the body of peer reviewed research addressing the potential impacts of their unique brand of sound is sparse and particularly unsettled. Anecdotal evidence strongly suggests a connection between turbines and a constellation of symptoms including nausea, vertigo, blurred vision, unsteady movement, and difficulty reading, remembering, and thinking. The polarizing issue of wind-turbine noise is often framed one of two ways: Turbines are either harmless, or they tend to have powerful adverse effects, especially for sensitive individuals. According to Jim Cummings, Executive director of the nonprofit Acoustic Ecology Institute in Santa Fe, New Mexico, most of the reports to date that have concluded turbines are harmless examined "direct" effects of sound on people and tended to discount "indirect" effects moderated by annoyance, sleep disruption, and associated stress. But research that considered indirect pathways has yielded evidence strongly suggesting the potential for harm.[87]

Consider the conclusions of another study published in *Noise and Health.*:

We report a cross-sectional study comparing the health-related quality of life (HRQOL) of individuals residing in the proximity of a wind farm to those residing in a demographically matched area sufficiently displaced from wind turbines. The study employed a nonequivalent comparison group posttest-only design. Self-administered

---

[86] D.J. Bennett, B. Atkinson, H. Bakker, R. Thorne, "Seismic Effects on Residents of 3 MW Wind Turbines," Proceedings from the Third International Meeting on Wind Turbine Noise (June 17-19, 2009). Note the study of seismic vibrations from wind turbines at 10 kilometers in Eskdalemuir Working Group, "Initial Study of Seismic Ground Vibration Data From Mega-Watt Class Wind Turbines" (June 2013).

[87] Nate Seltenrich, "Wind Turbines: A Different Kind of Noise?" *Environmental Health Perspectives* 122:1. A20 (2014).

questionnaires, which included the brief version of the World Health Organization quality of life scale, were delivered to residents in two adjacent areas in semirural New Zealand. Participants were also asked to identify annoying noises, indicate their degree of noise sensitivity, and rate amenity. Statistically significant differences were noted in some HRQOL domain scores, with residents living within 2 km of a turbine installation reporting lower overall quality of life, physical quality of life, and environmental quality of life. Those exposed to turbine noise also reported significantly lower sleep quality, and rated their environment as less restful. Our data suggest that wind farm noise can negatively impact facets of HRQOL.[88]

In short, the scientists confirm a lower quality of life for nearby residents. This general conclusion is affirmed by comments in *The Canadian Family Physician*:

Industrial wind turbines can harm human health if sited too close to residents… The documented symptoms are usually stress disorder–type diseases acting via indirect pathways and can represent serious harm to human health.[89]

This conclusion is also supported in a 2012 article published in *Noise and Health*:

Industrial wind turbine noise is a further source of environmental noise, with the potential to harm human health. Current regulations seem to be insufficient to adequately protect the human population living close to IWTs. Our research suggests that adverse effects are observed at distances even beyond 1 km.[90]

The evidence for negative health effects from wind turbines is so strong that scientists and scholars have had to appeal to new or specialized

---

[88] Daniel Shepherd, David McBride, David Welch, Erin Hill, "Evaluating the impact of wind turbine noise on health-related quality of life," *Noise and Health* 13:54 (2011): 333-339.

[89] Roy Jeffrey, Carmen Krogh, Brett Horner, "Adverse Health Effects of Industrial Wind Turbines," *Canadian Family Physician* 59:5 (2013).

[90] Michael Nissenbaum, Jeffrey Armanini, Christopher Hanning, "Effects of industrial wind turbine noise on sleep and health," *Noise and Health* 14:60 (2012): 237-243.

vocabulary. This includes "Wind Turbine Syndrome" (WTS) and "Vibroacoustic Disease" (VAD). On this second title, three audiologists explain what VAD really amounts to:

> ...some researchers are referring to these effects as Vibroacoustic Disease, or VAD (Castelo Branco, 1999; Castelo Branco and AlvesPereira, 2004). VAD is described as occurring in persons who are exposed to high-level (>90 dB SPL) infra- and low-frequency noise (ILFN), under 500 Hz, for periods of 10 years or more. It is believed to be a systemic pathology characterized by direct tissue damage to a variety of bodily organs and may involve abnormal proliferation of extracellular matrices.[91]

Max Whisson summarizes the problem with VAD—but in much more alarming and serious terms:

> Much of what has been discovered over the last three decades is reported by Mariana Alves-Pereira and Nuno Castelo Branco of Portugal. These extensive studies report numerous serious illnesses and, yes, many deaths, mainly from unusual cancers. A particularly characteristic finding is a thickening of the fibrous sheath surrounding the heart, the pericardium. Diseases such as type I diabetes and epilepsy developing late in life were also found and unusual malignant tumours were seen in the lungs, colon and brain. Rage attacks occurred in some individuals and sudden attacks of nonconvulsive mental defects were seen. These illnesses were caused by low frequency vibrations and developed slowly over many years, with deaths usually occurring after five years of exposure. The low frequency induced disease complex is called Vibro Acoustic Disease, or VAD and is thought to be the result of disruption of the fine fibres that connect the cells of the body. This disease complex is not yet widely recognised clinically or legally and this has seriously delayed diagnosis. Detailed experimental studies of VAD pathology have been reported. A characteristic finding is the production of excess collagen in the absence of an inflammatory response. This results in the thickening of blood vessel walls and abnormal gas flow in

---

[91] Jerry Punch, Richard James, and Dan Pabst, "Wind Turbine Noise: What Audiologists Should Know," *Audiology Today* (July-August 2010): 24.

the lungs. Other findings in the experimental studies were unusual cell death without the usual cell suicide mechanism of apoptosis.[92]

Long term exposure to infrasound leads to cancer, mental defects, and tumors? This is not unreasonable—nor is it an isolated concern.

A report from 2009 prepared for the Wisconsin Public Service Commission explains the findings of numerous other studies on this topic:

> ...the effects of low frequency noise among 439 employees working in offices, laboratories, and industries were also evaluated in another study. It was shown that there was a relationship between fatigue and tiredness after work and increasing low frequency noise. There were no employees that were exposed to low frequency noise with C-A differences greater than 20 dB (Schust M. 2004; Tesarz M. et al. 1997). Ising et al. conducted a study that examined the effect of low frequency nighttime traffic noise by measuring saliva cortisol concentrations in children. Based on a previous study, the authors stated that the full spectrum of truck noise in the children's bedroom was at a maximum of 100 Hz (Ising H. et al. 2004; Ising H. and Kruppa B. 2004). It was found that the children under high noise exposure (8h = 54-70dB(A)) had a significantly increased morning saliva cortisol concentration compared to a control population, which indicated an activation of the hypothalamus-pituitary-adrenal (HPA) axis (Ising H. et al. 2004). This endocrine change was found to be an indication of restless sleep and a further aggravation of bronchitis in the children. Finally, in 2000, a multidisciplinary group of clinicians and researchers called the Study Group on Neonatal Intensive Care Unit (NICU) Sound and the Expert Panel gathered and reviewed over 50 studies on the effects of sound on the fetus, newborn, and preterm infants. Upon the completion of review, the panel recommended that women should avoid prolonged exposure to low frequency sound levels (< 250 Hz) above 65 dB(A) during pregnancy (Graven SN. 2000). This recommendation was based on research that was conducted on sheep fetuses, which determined that after sustained periods of intense low frequency sound, the fetuses

---

[92] Max Whisson, "Wind Power and Ecology," *Nature and Society* (November-October 2011).

experienced injury to the hair cells of cochlea (Graven SN. 2000).[93]

Consider, also, an article from *Audiology Today:*

> …there is increasingly clear evidence that audible and low-frequency acoustic energy from these turbines is sufficiently intense to cause extreme annoyance and inability to sleep, or disturbed sleep, in individuals living near them. Jung and colleagues (2008), in a Korean study, concluded that low-frequency noise in the frequency range above 30 Hz can lead to psychological complaints and that infrasound in the frequency range of 5–8 Hz can cause complaints due to rattling doors and windows in homes.[94]

This is confirmed in other articles, such as the following:

> …there are now numerous reports (e.g. Pierpont 2009; Punch et al, 2010) discussed extensively in this journal that are highly suggestive that individuals living near wind turbines are made ill, with a plethora of symptoms which commonly include chronic sleep disturbance. The fact that such reports are being dismissed on the grounds that the level of infrasound produced by wind turbines is at too low a level to be heard appears to totally ignore the known physiology of the ear. Pathways from the OHC to the brain exist by which infrasound that cannot be consciously perceived could influence other subconscious functions.[95]

The point is clear: long-term exposure to low-frequency sound can be *very dangerous.*

Wind developers often reply by saying "what you can't hear can't hurt you." As some of the scientists indicate above, this is hopelessly naïve. We could say the same about nuclear radiation—which is also silent and invisible. Is anyone really going to argue that long-term exposure to

---

[93] Mark Roberts, et. al., "Evaluation of the Scientific Literature on the Health Effects Associated with Wind Turbines and Low Frequency Sound." Prepared for Wisconsin Public Service Commission (2009), 35-36.
[94] Punch et. al, "Wind Turbine Noise," 24.
[95] Salt and Kaltenbach, "Infrasound from Wind Turbines."

nuclear radiation is "harmless"? I don't think so.[96]

But it gets worse. *The infrasound caused by wind turbines is worse than from other sources.* Why? Because the sound waves are inconsistent. This is referred to as "amplitude modulation." In a 2014 study published by the Acoustical Society of America, the authors say:

> Our research has suggested a number of mechanisms by which low-frequency noise could bother individuals living near wind turbines: causing endolymphatic hydrops, exciting subconscious pathways, and amplitude modulation of audible sounds. Here we focus on the latter mechanism, amplitude modulation... Our results suggest that that infrasound generated by wind turbines may cause amplitude modulation of audible sounds, which is often the basis for complaints from those living near wind turbines.[97]

This is confirmed by audiologists...

> Studies carried out in Denmark, The Netherlands, and Germany (Wolsink and Sprengers, 1993; Wolsink et al, 1993), a Danish study (Pedersen and Nielsen, 1994), and two Swedish studies (Pedersen and Persson Waye, 2004, 2007) collectively indicate that wind turbines differ from other sources of community noise in several respects. These investigators confirm the findings of earlier research that amplitude-modulated sound is more easily perceived and more annoying than constant-level sounds (Bradley, 1994; Bengtsson et al, 2004) and that sounds that are unpredictable and uncontrollable are more annoying than other sounds (Geen and McCown, 1984; Hatfield et al, 2002).[98]

This is also given concern in the *Bulletin of Science, Technology, and Society*:

---

[96] Oddly, then, "Leventhall (2006) changed his position, stating that although wind turbines do produce significant levels of low-frequency sound, they do not pose a threat to humans—in effect reverting to the notion that what you can't hear can't hurt you." Punch et. al., "Wind Turbine Noise," 26.

[97] Jeffry Lichtenhan and Alec Salt, "Amplitude modulation of audible sounds by non-audible sounds," *Proceedings of Meetings on Acoustics*. Published by Acoustical Society of America. Vol 19 (2014).

[98] Punch et. al., "Wind Turbine Noise," 23.

...given the amplitude modulation, the allowed intrusion above ambient is far too high; there is no account taken of uncertainty in the prediction of noise at a home; there is no account taken for the excess noise caused by turbulent inflow, both natural and up-wind turbine wake; and the lack of compliance testing leaves the adverse health effects to compound from one completed wind farm to the next one being designed.[99]

So it's not just that the noise and vibrations produced by wind turbines is annoying and likely harmful—it's *especially* annoying and harmful. This means that residents and environmentalists should be *particularly concerned* about wind farms being erected over thousands of square miles of inhabited land.

But it gets even worse still.

Infrasound and its effects are *amplified* by the size of the turbine—and any developer will tell you (truthfully this time) that the trend is to build turbines bigger and bigger as projects go on. 1.85MW towers at 300-400ft tall used to be the standard, but now 3MW at 550ft tall are becoming the new standard. All of this is bad news—as reported in the prestigious *Journal of Acoustical Society in America*:

> The relative amount of low-frequency noise is higher for large turbines (2.3–3.6 MW) than for small turbines ($\leq$ 2 MW), and the difference is statistically significant. The difference can also be expressed as a downward shift of the spectrum of approximately one-third of an octave. A further shift of similar size is suggested for future turbines in the 10-MW range. Due to the air absorption, the higher low-frequency content becomes even more pronounced, when sound pressure levels in relevant neighbor distances are considered.[100]

It is no surprise, then, that a French study conducted back in 2004 suggested that the proper setback to avoid these negative effects "must not be sited less than 5 km (3.1 miles) from all habitation, because of the

---

[99] John Harrison, "Wind Turbine Noise," *Bulletin of Science, Technology, and Society* 31:256 (2011): 12.
[100] C. Pedersen and Henrich Moller, "Low-frequency Noise from Large Wind Turbines," *Journal of Acoustical Society in America* 129:6 (2011): 3727-3744.

risks produced by infrasound."[101] Wind developers are reluctant to set back the towers more than a mile. Most or many try to force a 1,000 ft setback down the throats of residents. This is almost certainly unsafe.

By far, the most common symptom of negative health-effects is *losing sleep*. Here, the hard-data is more conclusive. In a 2008 study done through the University of Gothenburg, the authors conclude that:

> At high levels of wind turbine sound (more than 45 dBA) interruption of sleep was more likely than at low levels. Higher levels of background sound from road traffic also increased the odds for interrupted sleep. Annoyance from wind turbine sound was related to difficulties with falling asleep and to higher stress scores.[102]

In another study:

> In total, seventy two percent of participants reported either increased symptoms of anxiety, stress, or depression since the start of their local wind project (Table 1)… Among study participants, the most common adverse health outcomes reported included sleep disturbance, excessive tiredness, and headaches.[103]

And in another study:

> We conclude that the noise emissions of IWTs disturbed the sleep and caused daytime sleepiness and impaired mental health in residents living within 1.4 km of the two IWT installations studied.[104]

And then in a 2016 study:

---

[101] A translated summary of the French study by Marjolaine Villey-Migraine, "EFFETS DE L'EOLIEN INDUSTRIEL SUR LA SANTE DES HOMMES." Université Paris II-Panthéon-Assas, 2004.

[102] E. Pederson, et. al. "Windfarm Perception: Visual and acoustic impact of wind turbine farms on residents," University of Gothenburg (2008), 4.

[103] Knopper and Christopher Ollson, "Health Effects."

[104] Michael Nissenbaum, Jeffrey Armanini, Christopher Hanning. "Effects of industrial wind turbine noise on sleep and health," *Noise and Health* 14:60. (2012): 237-243.

The study further shows that the noise emitted by wind turbines is clearly not the only annoying feature attributed to wind turbines. Annoyance with wind turbines was also related to visual impacts, shadow flicker, and blinking lights. Participants were also found to be concerned for their physical safety. That concern, in turn, was related to annoyance. These findings imply that amelioration of community reactions to wind turbines should consider these factors collectively.[105]

Of course, none of these studies were necessary in the first place. All that a person had to do is go to a wind farm and ask the surrounding residents how their sleep has changed, and many or most (at least those who aren't aware or don't care about their confidentiality contract!) would tell you: *"I'm not sleeping as good as I used to."* But because Big Wind has placed the burden of proof on the residents, dissenters have to prove that they're not "making stuff up."

Unsurprisingly, then, when scholars review all the relevant literature, they come to the same basic conclusion: *wind farms ruin people's sleep.* In a 2014 review article in the journal *PLoS One*, we read that, "Exposure to wind turbines does seem to increase the risk of annoyance and self-reported sleep disturbance in a dose-response relationship."[106] In another review of the literature, "…it is acknowledged that noise from wind turbines can be annoying to some and associated with some reported health effects (e.g., sleep disturbance), especially when found at sound pressure levels greater than 40 db(A)…"[107]

Most of the above studies have to do with the effects of "infrasound" and VAD and its effects. But what about *audible* sound? Are wind farms actually "noisy," and does this negatively affect people's experience?

Again, the answer is an obvious "yes." Hundreds of peoples' ears are not lying to them (surprise!). But, again, because Big Wind has put the world on the defensive, studies have had to be published just to prove that

---

[105] Christina Ioannidou, Sébastien Santurette and Cheol-Ho Jeong, "Effect of modulation depth, frequency, and intermittence on wind turbine noise annoyance," Journal of Acoustiscal Society of America 139:1241 (2016).
[106] Jesper Schmidt and Mads Klokker, "Health Effects Related to Wind Turbine Noise Exposure: A Systematic Review," *PLoS One* 9:12 (2014).
[107] Loren Knopper and Christopher Ollson, "Health effects and wind turbines: A review of the literature," *Environmental Health* 10:78 (2011).

peoples' ears actually work.

One report from Australia concluded that "Six studies assessed the association of annoyance with exposure to estimated wind farm noise or proximity to a wind farm. The studies all reported an association between annoyance and higher estimated levels of wind farm noise or living closer to a wind farm."[108] In another article, we read that:

> Wind turbines are noisy and cause annoyance in about 20% of residents living within a distance considered acceptable by regulatory authorities. For many of this 20% the annoyance and sleep disturbance leads on to adverse health effects. This is a far larger proportion than for those living with traffic and industrial noise at the same level. The annoyance and adverse health effects are attributable to the character of turbine noise and to deficiencies in noise regulations.[109]

### Other Health Effects

Another negative effect on human life from wind energy is shadow-flicker. This effect is more pronounced in less foggy and rainy climates—like the sunny Midwest. Half the sunlight of a single day shines on land at a significant angle. This casts longer and longer shadows from tall objects as the sun approaches the horizon. Because wind towers are so huge, they cast shadows for *hundreds of feet*. People living in cities know what this is like, and how shadows limit the amount of sunlight in a day and can effect a number of things (planning for building location, the type of plants that will grow in the shade, etc.). But it's much more complicated than this for wind turbines because the shadows are *rapidly moving*.[110]

---

[108] Australian National Health and Medical Research Council. "Information Paper: Evidence on Wind Farms and Human Health," (February, 2015), 18.
[109] Harrison, "Wind Turbine Noise," 12.
[110] The photo below comes from Ben VanderVeen at http://www.benvanderveen.com/400-feet-up/

Videos of this annoying "shadow-flicker" can be found on YouTube and elsewhere. Calm evenings in the backyard are no longer calm, but instead homeowners experience a dizzying, strobe-light flicker of lights passing over acres and acres of land.

It goes without saying that there is no one who would want this kind of environmental chaos on their house or their backyard. It is a clear violation of the right to enjoy one's own property. And it also goes without saying that this may easily qualify as a "negative health effect."

In fact, a laboratory experiment modeling this effect resulted in the following results, published by the Australian National Health and Medical Research Council: "People exposed for short periods to simulated wind turbine shadow flicker in a laboratory have shown some evidence of impaired cognition and a physiological stress response."[111] Again, this is obvious and no evidence is needed. But the "hard evidence" is there anyway.

---

[111] Australian National Health and Medical Research Council. "Information Paper: Evidence on Wind Farms and Human Health," (February, 2015), 23.

## Big Wind's Decisive "Refutation" of Negative Health Effects?

Big Wind's back is against the wall. They're now surrounded by audiologists, physicians, scientists, and professors who are shaking their heads about wind farms being "safe." What has been their response?

Their response was predictable: host an artificial panel with credentialed experts, and get them to say that (contrary to the mountain of evidence) wind turbines are completely safe. Then, use this event as definite "proof" (and criticize anyone who disagrees with "the experts").

This essentially happened in 2009. The AWEA prepared an "Expert Panel Review" called "Wind Turbine Sound and Health Effects." Their opinions? A simple denial:

> In particular, the panel considered "wind turbine syndrome" and vibroacoustic disease, which have been claimed as causes of adverse health effects. The evidence indicates that "wind turbine syndrome" is based on misinterpretation of physiologic data and that the features of the so-called syndrome are merely a subset of annoyance reactions.[112]

To gain better credibility, these conclusions had to be published. So the same authors (who were conveniently selected from the prestigious MIT) published their "research" in *The Journal of Occupational and Environmental Medicine*, selectively arranging even the most disturbing data into the most favorable conclusions.[113] The publication was explicitly "funded by the Canadian wind energy association, CanWEA, and the European Wind Energy Association (EWEA)." Yet, the public is supposed to believe it's "unbiased."[114]

The authors concluded that:

---

[112] W. David Colby, Robert Dobie, Robert McCunney, et. al. "Wind Turbine Sound and Health Effects," An Expert Panel Review 2009, Prepared for American Wind Energy Association and Canadian Wind Energy Association.

[113] Robert McCunney, et. al., "Wind Turbines and Health: A Critical Review of the Scientific Literature," *Journal of Occupational and Environmental Medicine* 56:11 (November 2014): 108-130.

[114] EWEA, "Wind turbines not a risk to human health, says MIT study." (March 12, 2014).

1. Measurements of low-frequency sound, infrasound, tonal sound emission, and amplitude-modulated sound show that infrasound is emitted by wind turbines. The levels of infrasound at customary distances to homes are typically well below audibility thresholds.

2. No cohort or case–control studies were located in this updated review of the peer-reviewed literature. Nevertheless, among the cross-sectional studies of better quality, no clear or consistent association is seen between wind turbine noise and any reported disease or other indicator of harm to human health.

3. Components of wind turbine sound, including infrasound and low-frequency sound, have not been shown to present unique health risks to people living near wind turbines.

4. Annoyance associated with living near wind turbines is a complex phenomenon related to personal factors. Noise from turbines plays a minor role in comparison with other factors in leading people to report annoyance in the context of wind turbines.[115]

Big Wind now had exactly what it had needed for so many years.

The headlines went crazy. Website after website and newspaper after newspaper ran triumphant titles: "MIT Study: Wind Farms Do Not Harm Human Health," "Wind Turbines are no health risk," "No health impacts from wind turbine noise, says MIT study," "Wind farms cause no harm to human health: MIT study," "MIT finds no human health risk from wind turbines," and on it went.

If only the media reported the truth.

There are a host of obvious problems with the whole project. First, *the article wasn't a quantitative "study."* It was a *literature review.* No data was collected. No field research was conducted. No original surveys were distributed, collected, and analyzed. The authors simply surveyed some of the actual studies and then drew their own conclusions about what they said. This is important to keep in mind, because this makes it very easy to select and give weight to only the studies that fit a particular conclusion—and criticize the inadequacy of studies that don't. (This is precisely what the article does.)

Second, *it was funded by two national lobbyist-groups for wind energy.* This was anything but "independent research"—despite what the EWEA press

---

[115] Ibid.

release reported. Everyone knows that if you've been bought, you're owned.

Third, *each one of the four conclusions (quoted above) is carefully crafted to avoid the main issues and evidence.* Refer back to earlier sections of this chapter regarding what "evidence" counts.

> *"If you've been bought, you're owned."*

Fourth, *the article claims that it is purely academic, citing only peer-review academic literature, but there are exceptions hidden in the paper.* One exception includes the following: "One study published as part of a conference proceedings did not meet the peer-reviewed journal eligibility criterion but was included because it seemed to be the first epidemiological study on this topic and an impetus for subsequent studies."[116] Or was it included because of its convenient conclusions? I think this is a legitimate question to ask, because this exception source suggests that "noise-related annoyance was weakly correlated with objective sound levels but more strongly correlated with indicators of respondents' attitudes and personality."[117] The authors repeat this idea in their conclusion to the section. It just seems slightly convenient to include this particular exception.

Fifth, *there are lots of problems with the study itself.* Consider the following quote from the paper:

A Canadian report investigated the total number of noise-related complaints because of operating wind farms in Alberta, Canada, over its entire history of wind power. Wind power capacity exceeds 1100 MW; some of the turbines have been in operation for 20 years. Five noise-oriented complaints at utility-scale wind farms were reported over this period, none of which were repeated after the complaints were addressed.[118]

The authors have apparently forgotten that landowners typically sign a gag-order that forbids them from complaining. (So, yes, we would expect

---

[116] Ibid.
[117] Ibid.
[118] Ibid.

the number of complaints to be small.) This legal variable alone throws off entire chunks of the paper. So much for being a "critical" review!

Another uncritical observation is that "Annoyance does not correlate well or at all with objective sound measurements or calculated sound pressures."[119] An implication here is that we can't say that people will get annoyed if something gets louder and louder. But, this makes no sense. If a stereo is quietly playing music but I crank it up to 50 decibels, then 100, then 150, then 200, *everyone* would be "annoyed" (and probably deaf). This is true regardless if we have "evidence" of this or not. Just because "annoyance" is a relative concept doesn't mean it can't be associated with noise.

The authors also claim that the noise from wind turbines isn't much different than listening to ocean waves or your furnace fan: "the phenomena that constitute wind turbine exposures—primarily noise and visual effect—are not dissimilar to many other environmental (eg, noise of waves along shorelines) and anthropogenic (eg., noise from indoor Heating Ventilation and Air Conditioning or road traffic) stimuli, for which research and practical experience indicate no direct harm to human health."[120] This just isn't the case—as audiologists have demonstrated in the studies observed above in this chapter; wind turbine noise *does* have distinctive features.

But there is something even more problematic in this argument: the appeal to "practical experience." Why are these academics permitted to appeal to "practical experience" when those actually living under wind turbines are not? Because practical experience would suggest that living beside dozens of massive vibrating, rotating skyscrapers buried deep into the ground and towering high into the air is probably not very "healthy" for anyone. Critics of wind energy aren't allowed to say this because it's "unscientific" and not "evidence-based." Yet, here it is in the peer-reviewed article.

> *"Why are these academics permitted to appeal to 'practical experience' when those actually living under wind turbines are not?"*

---

[119] Ibid.
[120] Ibid.

And then there is also the interesting claim that "Economic benefit mitigates the effect of wind turbine sound." This simple claim is unqualified except in the following sentence that "research is needed to clarify the potential confounding role of (self)selection in this finding." Thus, the authors consider it a generally-accepted fact that (though needing more research) apparently *whatever* negative health effects may occur from wind turbines, cash will fix it. While there is probably truth that landowners getting royalties are less "annoyed" than those who aren't getting royalties, this is still incredible. Would the authors suggest that simply handing out money can cure dizziness and sleeplessness? Perhaps, though we're not told. (What kind of "science" is this?)

Sixth, the conclusions of any literature review are never definitive and absolute. It is a fallible snapshot in time. As more and more studies are conducted, conclusions might change. This means that even if this paper and all of its conclusions *were* sound, it is only *temporary and open for criticism.* It is impossible to claim that any research—especially a single paper— "settles the matter" once and for all.

Yet, that is precisely what the Public Affairs Director of Wind Europe claims: "These results should lay to rest any concerns that some citizens may have with regard to living near wind turbines."[121] Lay to rest? Wide-awake more like!

In the end, the definitive "MIT Study" that "proves" that wind energy is safe is just another bluff. Only here the bluff is not "everyone is signed up." The bluff is "all the experts and evidence says that wind energy is green and safe."

Hot air, indeed. Within a year, the legitimacy of the article was refuted in the same journal.[122] These more level-headed scientists made a number of important points—many that I've already covered above. For example, they write that, "McCunney et al seem to have affirmed the all-too-common tendency to misinterpret the lack of evidence as proof of the absence of direct AHEs [Adverse Health Effects]." Exactly! Furthermore, "It appears that in Canada, the United States, the UK, and

---

[121] Iván Pineda, in EWEA, "Wind Turbines Not a Risk."
[122] Murray May, Robert McMurtry, "Wind Turbines and Adverse Health Effects: A Second Opinion," *Journal of Occupational and Environmental Medicine* 57:10 (October 2015):e130-e132.

Australia, industry literature reviews have interpreted the word 'annoyance' to mean a minor inconvenience...their review seems preoccupied with personality factors." Yes again!

If all of this qualifies as cutting edge "science," it is truly a pitiful situation, indeed.

## Conclusion

I wrote a letter to the editor last year comparing "Wind Turbine Syndrome" (WTS) to tobacco, asbestos, and Agent Orange. All of these were classic icons of products that negatively impacted one's health—but were covered up for years by the government and crony-capitalists that made billions. Eventually the word got out, and they all ended up in lawsuits and many innocent lives were lost.

Wind Turbine Syndrome and Vibro-Acoustic Disease will probably be the same thing. It won't immediately kill people, and everybody that lives close to a wind turbine won't necessarily suffer from it. But many do, and the destructive, long-term effects have yet to be seen.

And this goes beyond human effects.

We return to the subject of the environment. One of my classmates that lives near a wind project reports that ever since the project got started, "the deer are gone." There was also testimony at the Avon PUC meeting that when dogs were transported through the wind farm, they were uneasy and apparently affected by the turbines, because when they drove a different route, the dogs were more comfortable and normal.

But maybe all this is made-up, too. Maybe the deer and dogs have gone "hysterical" over the inconvenience of having wind turbines around their kennels and pastures. Perhaps their "personality" is the problem.

You can decide.

# — 10 —

# Conclusion

The major conclusions of this book have already been summarized in the last chapter, and they don't need to be revisited here. Furthermore, these conclusions are fairly straightforward and need little by way of review.

How, then, to conclude our journey through the blades of wind energy?

I want to conclude with the same topic I began with: the quality of life in rural living.

## The Future of Rural Living

The AP reported in the *Mitchell Daily Republic* in April of 2015 that there are up to 30,000 additional wind turbines being planned for Montana, Iowa, Minnesota, Nebraska, and North and South Dakota. As of that time, there were already about 8,600 wind turbines in these states. As of this writing, there are 35 proposed industrial wind projects in South Dakota, in addition to the 13 that are already here. In one of Prevailing Winds brochures we read about 100 towers on approximately 36,000 acres of land. Using that ratio, 360 acres for one tower (times 38,600 towers), that's *fourteen million acres of pristine rural landscape destroyed by industrial wind energy projects.* This isn't even to mention the reduction in the quality of life for all of the *residents* that would live within these 14 million acres.

The questions at this point are:

1. How do we choose to live, what do we want our state to look like and what will be left of our beautiful state if we continue to let these wind turbines be built by the hundreds or thousands?

2. Are the county zoning boards, the commissioners, the state legislators, the Governor, and (in South Dakota's case) our 3 representatives in Washington D.C. going to become or continue to be part of this scam?

The wind farm scam will run until the PTC money runs out. But efforts are already under way to subvert the PTC phase out.

We should be reminded that the country is *20 trillion dollars* in debt. Even if by some miracle this could be brought down to zero in the next half-century, that would still mean that the government is *dead cash broke*. Are we naïve enough to think that the taxpayer is going to fund these wind turbines till the end of time while the whole rural United States of America becomes one giant industrial park?

The point here is that when taxpayer money runs out and the wind projects are continually losing money, what good are they to anybody? And what do we want our state to look like? Spain? Denmark? Germany? If you are now fortunate enough to live in rural South Dakota, instead of stepping outside early in the morning to hear the flight of geese migrating on top of the sound of crickets in the thicket, do you want to hear the *whoosh whoosh* of wind turbines? Are you going to step outside one last time before bedtime to gaze at the stars and thank God one more time for this wonderful place to live—but instead of stars see hundreds of red blinking lights bordering the horizon?

None of this is a romantic exaggeration. Not in the least. If you have not yet had the opportunity to drive in an industrial wind project of over 50 towers, make an effort to do so. Get out of the car and imagine that place as your new home.

Because unless something changes, this is precisely the situation that's coming—to a field and rural setting near you.

There are two simple ways to stop this devastation of rural America. For South Dakota in particular, the most effective (and easiest) way is refusing to sign leases or easements offered by developers. This easily preserves the land. Second, County officials should educate themselves on the negatives of wind energy and understand the taxpayer scam that it is. They should refuse to deal with these developers, or at the very least provide setbacks of 2-3 miles from any residence to protect their people. (Either one of these scenarios would send the developer down the road to sell their snake oil to somebody else.)

On the state-level of legislation, it would be great to see four things considered for policy—none of which are very demanding at all:

1. Any landowner that signs a wind easement/lease should have 30 days to reconsider.

2. The South Dakota Real Estate Commission should add "the existence or knowledge of any present or future wind farm" in the South Dakota Real Estate property disclosure. This would protect any homebuyer from finding out after it's too late that they will be living in an industrial wind park.

3. The state should put into law minimum setbacks from residences of 2 miles (or more) and 1000 ft. from a property line. Waivers would be available to participants in wind energy unless it infringes upon a neighbor's setback.

4. The state should make the wind project developer pay for any loss in value to a homeowner because of the presence of a wind energy system.

I get frustrated when people tell me "I think I'll just stay neutral," or "I don't want to get involved." This attitude is better than blind obedience to developers, politicians, or otherwise. But this only works for so long. Who can live a completely "neutral" life? And why would one want to? Do we not have convictions worth acting upon?

## Final Words

The general purpose of this book was to educate those who have had little or no knowledge of the negative features of wind energy. While I have much more to learn myself, I hope it has at least opened your eyes to a different perspective.

And if you have read this whole book and are still skeptical, I invite you to do the following to help you "get off the fence":

1. Talk to some people that live under wind turbines that have not signed up or invested. Remember, the people that have signed up may have to abide by the confidentiality clause and not complain.
2. When you encounter a real animate pro-wind person, ask them what their interest in the industry is? Are they an investor? Do they sell concrete? Are they working for the AWEA or South Dakota Wind Energy Association? Have they sold their easements/leases?
3. Again, drive through a wind project of 50 turbines or more, stop and listen. Ask yourself if you would like to live there.
4. Pay attention to national politics, especially the budget. Listen closely to the lobbying that is already taking place to rescind the PTC phase out. If wind energy is so great, and becoming so efficient and cheap, why would they be asking to extend the PTC?
5. Go to YouTube for some personal testimonies of people living under wind projects.

In short, get educated now or you will certainly get educated later. Do your share in keeping South Dakota (or whatever state you may live in) the beautiful place that it is. Don't put money ahead of you or your neighbor's quality of life. And thank the Lord every night that you have been chosen to live in one of the greatest places on the planet.

# Appendix A:
## Testimonies

The following testimonies are a selection of local witnesses who have gotten involved with wind farms one way or another. Most were written within the last two years. Most were directly sent to me.

---

In April of 2010, my husband Mike and I flew from California, where we had lived all of our lives, to South Dakota to look at a property that seemed to fit our dream for our retirement. The 8 acre, 100 year old farmstead had everything we had planned for and dreamed of. We made an offer on the property and it was accepted. We returned to California to work the last nine months of 31 and 25-year careers.

April 2011 we began living here, excited to have realized our lifelong dream. We invested in a new roof and remodeled the kitchen as both were in poor condition. We had plans for more improvements until when, in November of 2013, we learned a wind farm was about to be constructed to the west of us and the closest turbines would be only three miles from our property. The reality set in and we dropped our plans to invest in more improvements to our home and property. The recent plan of more turbines to be added to the existing wind farm has reinforced our decision.

We had already witnessed the devastating effects wind farms had on the landscapes of California, Minnesota, and Iowa. We would never have considered looking at, much less purchasing a property with a wind farm proposed to be built near it or within view of it. Any knowledge of the wind farm was not disclosed to us in the real estate transaction. Once we had purchased and moved here we became acquainted with many people in the area. Of all the people we met, only one, told us about the wind farm, and said it would be built near Avon, SD which is about twenty miles from our home. I happened to see the public notice regarding a hearing for Conditional Use Permits in the paper with the compass coordinates being nearly the same as our property. Though I attended that hearing and another hearing for additional permits, it was clear, the decision had been made and Mike and I had no recourse whatsoever.

It has been hugely disappointing to have our dream property with stunning views change forever. Perhaps even more disappointing is the way it was done, with secrecy and deceit, and lack of concern for the many people like us who are negatively affected by living near an industrial wind farm.

Karen Jenkins, April 2017
**Tripp, SD**

---

I was and still on Holt counties zoning and planning board. On the week of the vote on this wind farm, we received a binder providing info on the project. I, along with of the board members, did not do our research. This info is a one way road for the wind projects. That night I ask specific questions regarding location of towers and noise issues. The answers I received were all lies. At the time I believed the rep. When the vote came my gut said to vote no, and I did not. This is a regret I will have to live with forever. The commissioners were looking at all the "money" for the county. Not so. We were told the towers would not be closer than 4-5 miles; they are 1 3/8 miles from our home. They also said we would not hear them, we do when we are on the back side or the down wind direction. The sound is disturbing to our peaceful place.

Everybody needs to research other areas that have had wind towers in place for a while and the picture becomes very clear. They do not work and the damages caused to health, safety and welfare outweigh any benefits. I am an adjuster for Farm Bureau and will be traveling next week. If you or anyone else would like to come to our place and witness this ridiculous project just let us know. You are more than welcome.

Keith May, March 2017
**Holt County, Nebraska**

---

Hi, As a resident of Jerauld County and a landowner, a tenant of rented land, and the person who lives in a dwelling with 7 wind towers within a mile and as close as 1050 ft. from my house and the recipient of money from the towers that I live by I would hope you would take consideration of my opinions. The 1000 ft. setback is a joke after living by towers they just had well be 10 ft. from anything on my place. The negatives are what they are the noise and blinking lights are not stifled by a 1000 ft. plain and simple. It needs to be more distance. I wish it would've been a mile set back and then those who wouldn't mind the negatives of the towers could sign a waiver and let them closer to their property. I'm not against the wind energy industry I just didn't fully understand what the negatives were and now it's too late for me but that's why people evolve and learn from mistakes of the past and correct them for the future. There is a way too incorporate towers into communities but it's unfair to set them on or near people residences who don't want them and get all the bad and none of the good. I <u>do not</u> believe there will come a time when there is a tower on every quarter of land in a county. That would be the only way everyone would have the same good and bad of them. As it is now a few benefit and the rest don't. Thank you for your time.

Travis Krumvieda, April 2017
**Wessington Springs, SD**

---

South Dakota residents should think carefully before agreeing to give up tax revenue for the privilege of having their landscapes marred by thousands of massive mechanical machines and hundreds of miles of new transmission lines. I am from Colorado, but I have spent hundreds of hours driving through S.D., while commuting from Denver to southern Minnesota between 2007 and the present. Rather than traveling east on I-

80 and north on I-35, I always chose to travel north on Hwy. 83 from North Platte through the Sand Hills up to that "rare jewel" that is S.D. I would encounter only one wind turbine between the S.D. border and the Minnesota border. This turbine, now still and silent, was at the Rosebud Casino south of Mission. Too costly to remove, it will likely stand silent till the end of time. From Mission I would travel east, stopping at a farm near Winner for the night, where I would savor the evening sunset and the morning sunrise, marveling at the rare beauty of this still somewhat remote land. In the morning I would continue east and north to Chamberlain, across the Mighty Missouri and east on I-90, knowing that I could travel all the way to the Minnesota border without seeing a single massive turbine.

At the Minnesota border the view changed with the beginning of a 70 mile transmission line, constructed to carry power from the wind turbines that begin to appear. Thousands of miles of these new transmission lines have been built here in the U.S., the European Union and wherever these massive forests of spinning machines are erected. Further east on I-90 are mile after mile of wind turbines. The serenity of S.D. was gone. Iowa to the south is almost an impenetrable "forest" of wind turbines and transmission lines.

Beginning in 2007, I witnessed the rise of hundreds of wind turbines around Grand Meadow, Minn. They sprouted from the fertile farm fields, the "farmsteads" soon surrounded by giant propellers, the shadows and hum interrupting bacon and eggs in the morning and beef roast and mash potatoes and gravy in the evening. I was born about 15 miles from Grand Meadow, so I was very aware of the disappearing beauty. The name of the town did not lie. It truly was a "grand" meadow. It was being witness to the destruction of the original beauty that gave me the name of my book, "*Steal the Wind Reap the Whirlwind*," and the motivation to write it.

"Environmentalists" would, in times past, raise the alarm at obstructions being built by the thousands across the land, but today the "*Socio-Enviro-Emotionalists*" salivate at the site of these rising monsters, believing they are "saving the planet." Hundreds of groups have been formed to fight the "wind monster" here in the United States and in Canada, even more across Europe. Oklahoma is one state where residents are fighting back. Led by a now 87-year-old who wished to retire to his ranch, only to find that a wind farm was going to be built adjacent to his property, a non-profit was formed to take on the powerful wind industry. The website "windwaste.com" describes the hundreds of millions in lost taxes and the impact, especially on education, a cause he fought for his entire life. In his November 2015 email to me, he stated that Oklahoma was 1,000 teachers short in the public schools and the teachers had not had a raise since 2008. South Dakotans should study the battle and the progress of this group before submitting to the power of the wind industry.

Western European countries are vast forests of "Spinning Skyscrapers." Germany, in particular, is a "symbol" of the madness of replacing "active" power sources with variable "passive" power. Its "*Energiewende*" (energy transformation) program will cost more than one trillion Euros. At 1.79 times the size of S.D., more than 5,000 miles of new or extended transmission lines are being built to milk about 25,000 turbines. Germany has shut down eight of 17 "*zero-emissions*" nuclear plants and plans to shut down the remaining plants by 2022. It has also shut down a number of "new" natural gas plants. As a result, its $CO_2$ emissions have remained level or slightly increased since 2010, in spite of the tremendous investments in "renewable" energy. It has even been necessary to build new coal plants to stabilize the Pan-European grid.

Think carefully before you reduce your tax base and mar your pristine landscapes with these mechanical monsters. They will, in all likelihood, have a limited functional lifespan, but will mar the skyline for decades and beyond, too costly to dismantle, too difficult or impossible to recycle.

Duane Hyland, August 2016
**Golden, CO**
My Voice: Wind turbines to 'mar' horizon for eternity
*Duane, 82, of Golden, Colo., is retired having worked more than 50 years in the computer software field. He is the founder of three companies and author of the book "Steal the Wind Reap the Whirlwind."*

I made the biggest mistake of my life. I signed my farm for Wind Turbines and now I host two turbines.

Let me tell you about the total disregard these companies have for your land. After the first day of construction, I knew I was in big trouble. Different people every day, tearing my fields apart and driving anywhere they felt like. When digging these huge holes for the bases of the turbines, all this dirt and dead soil (they didn't haul any away). That dead soil was spread on top of the rest of my field. Stones and debris all left for me to clean up. Then there was all the ruts and compaction combined with roads through my fields; I now have which once was beautiful, healthy corn is now short and yellow. Erosion, improper drainage—didn't they say only a very small amount of land was to be used? Everything they tell you is a lie unless it's documented in writing. The second day I was told to go to my house and read my contract as I was told they owned the rights to my land as I had the right to watch and say nothing. I get paid $4,200.00 a year for each turbine, but take 37% for taxes, loss of crops.

That's pocket change left and no property rights.

I admit I made a huge mistake.

Al Hass, Hass Grain Farm, March 2016
**Malone, Wisconsin**

---

I am an associate real estate broker in Holt County, Nebraska. I have marketed and sold farms and ranches on a full time basis since 1987. I am not taking a stand for or against wind farms. What I would like to convey are the leases I have seen in Holt County, Nebraska. They have several flaws that are not in favor of the land owner.

1.  Confidentiality Clause: Prohibits the lessee and landowner from making any part of the lease available to a third party without the written consent of each party. Representing a seller of land with a lease prohibits us from furnishing lease to prospective buyers. We asked if we could have a confidentiality agreement signed by prospective buyers so they could read lease or allow their legal counsel to provide an opinion of lease. The answer

was "no" we were allowed to disclose that it was a 20 year lease only and nothing more. We could not give a buyer the lease agreement until after closing. In other words a buyer would have to assume any adverse conditions or liability the lease would cause. Most well-informed buyers would not consider assuming a lease without knowing the terms, conditions, and rental rates.

2. One does have to ask whys this agreement is so confidential.
3. Why would they not want others to read said lease.
4. Who would want to have a lease assigned to them that forbids prior legal counsel or knowledge of liability?
5. Each party shall be liable for disclosure of confidential information arrangements.
6. There are numerous areas of concern of said lease.
7. It is nearly impossible to market, sell or convey a property that has this limitation.
8. This is only one area of concern in leases we have read.

Robert Litz, March 2016
**Holt County, Nebraska**

---

Out of the 200 towers in the Prairie Breeze Project constructed by Invenergy in 2013-2016, I would guess that at least 25%, maybe more, have been taken down and repaired, several of them more than once. It takes 15-20 semi-trailers to haul in the crane. They have torn up many country roads because they don't care if they are muddy or not, simply using caterpillars to pull semis through the mud. Last year they even destroyed three county bridges while moving the cranes from one tower to another, making these roads unusable for 9 months. People that need to use these roads are at their mercy. It looks like wind towers are very poorly constructed and require lots and lots of maintaining. You may share this. People need to know what to expect with wind tower projects.

Gary Borer, June 2017
**Antelope County, Nebraska**

It took me about 2 years to adjust to the noise. Personal opinion, but I think the setback for a 3MW tower should be close to a mile. I have been told 2MW towers are only about half as loud. Closest tower to our house is 5/8 mile, and when wind direction is right with high humidity, we can hear the whoosh noise with windows closed and the TV on.

Dr. [chose not to disclose name], March 2015
**Bloomfield, Nebraska**

# Recommended Resources

**Books on Wind Energy**

Etherington, John. *The Wind Farm Scam*. London: Stacey International, 2009.

Pierpont, Nina. *Wind Turbine Syndrome: A Report on a Natural Experiment*. Santa Fe: K-Selected Books, 2009.

**Books on Economics**

DiLorenzo, Thomas. *The Problem With Socialism*. Washington D.C.: Regenery, 2016.

Friedman, Milton. *Capitalism and Freedom*. Chicago: University of Chicago Press, 2002.

Hazlitt, Henry. *Economics in One Lesson*. New York: Crown Business, 1988.

Mitchell, Matthew. *The Pathology of Privilege: The Economic Consequences of Government Favoritism*. Fairfax: Mercatus Center, 2015.

Ritenour, Shawn. *Foundations of Economics: A Christian View*. Eugene: Wipf and Stock, 2010.

Stroup, Richard. *Eco-Nomics: What Everyone Should Know About Economics and the Environment*. Washington D.C.: Cato Institute, 2003.

**Videos**

*Windfall*. Surge Media Canada. 2015.

*Downwind*. First Run Features. 2011. Awards:
   Official Selection, Toronto Film Festival
   Grand Prize Winner, DOC NYC

**Websites**

wind-watch.org

wiseenergy.org

windaction.org

coalitionforruralpropertyrights.com

we-caresd.org

caithnesswindfarms.co.uk/index.htm

edgarcountywatchdog.com